LIFE OF SCHAMYL.

LIFE OF SCHAMYL;

AND

NARRATIVE

OF THE

CIRCASSIAN WAR OF INDEPENDENCE AGAINST RUSSIA.

BY

J. MILTON MACKIE,

AUTHOR OF "COSAS DE ESPAÑA."

BOSTON:

PUBLISHED BY JOHN P. JEWETT AND COMPANY.

CLEVELAND, OHIO:

JEWETT, PROCTOR AND WORTHINGTON.

NEW YORK: SHELDON, LAMPORT AND BLAKEMAN.

1856.

CAMBRIDGE:
ALLEN AND FARNHAM, STEREOTYPERS AND PRINTERS.

PREFACE.

The principal authors who have recently written on Circassia are Bodenstedt, Moritz Wagner, Marlinski, Dubois de Montpéreux, Hommaire de Hell, Taillander, Marigny, Golovin, Bell, Longworth, Spencer, Knight, Cameron, Ditson; and from their pages chiefly has been filled the easel with the colors of which I have endeavored to paint the following picture of a career of heroism nowise inferior to that of the most famous champions of classical antiquity, of a war of independence such as may not improperly be compared with the most glorious struggles recorded in the annals of liberty, and of a state of society perhaps the most romantic and the most nearly resembling that described in the songs of Homer which the progress of civilization has now left for the admiration of mankind.

CONTENTS.

LIFE OF SCHAMYL.

I.

THE LAND OF SCHAMYL.

CIRCASSIA—under which name the country occupied by a great number of tribes of which the Circassians are one, is best known to foreigners—lies in the Caucasus, a range of mountains which, running in the direction between north-west and south-east, extends from the shores of the Black Sea to those of the Caspian, and divides by its wall of rock the two continents of Europe and Asia.

The traveller approaching these mountains from the steppes inhabited by the Cossacks subject to Russia, beholds at a distance of thirty miles a single white conical summit towering high above the otherwise level horizon. This is the peak of Elbrus, the loftiest in the Caucasian chain, and called by the natives the Dsching Padischah, or great spirit of the mountains. Next, is seen the no less solitary top of Kasbek, situated further eastward, and its snows tinged by the first red rays of the morning. Then, the whole line of summits, "the thousand peaked," rises to view; and finally, a lower range covered with forests, and hence called the Black Mountains, draws its dark and irregular outline against the higher snows beyond.

The waters shed from the northern declivities of the Caucasus, are received by two principal rivers, the Kuban and the Terek; while those which flow down on the south side are gathered into the Rion and the Kur, or ancient Cyrus. Of these streams the Kuban is the largest, and empties itself, as does the Rion, into the Black Sea; the other two running eastward to the Caspian.

The western portion more especially of the Black Mountains is heavily wooded. Gigantic oaks spread their branches above cliffs and summits, where in less favored climes only the cold pine would be able to find a scanty subsistence; while the spray of the Black Sea is dashed against the immense stems of the blood-wooded taxus, and the red and almond-leaved willows sweep with their long branches the waves. The box here is a giant of the forest; the stem of the juniper measures often fifteen feet in circumference; and the vine climbing to the top of the lofty elm sends its tendrils across to the neighboring beech, hanging festoons from tree-top to tree-top, and almost making of the forest one far spreading arbor. Lower down the pomegranate hangs out its blossoms; the fig and wild pear their fruits; the laurel and the myrtle their green leaves; while an infinite variety of creepers entwine themselves around every form, and wild flowering plants, from gorgeous rhododendrons and azalias to the lowly violet and arbutus, fill the woods with sweet odors.

The distant view of the Caucasus, so bold in its outlines and varied in its forms, surpasses in grandeur that of the Alps; and if from the small number of lakes and glaciers, the interior aspects present less of that exceeding beauty which characterizes the Swiss landscapes above those of all other mountains, there is nevertheless a brilliancy of tints in this oriental air, a glory of nearly five hundred miles of snow peaks, a luxuriance of woods on the lower ranges, and a degree of cultivation in the valleys where the hand of man has been busy since times the most remote, which render this mountain land one of the fairest portions of the globe, and worthy of having been, as by some traditions is reported, the cradle of the human race.

The western portion of the mountains is fruitful to the height of five thousand feet, and the eastern is frequently terraced with gardens. The valleys, green with meadows or golden with many varieties of grain, are dotted over with villages and clusters of cottages. White sheep in great numbers and jet black goats crop the hill-sides; while in lower pastures feed the buffalo and the camel. Herds of tame or half-wild horses roam at large through the glades; wild boars house among the reeds on the river banks; and the chamois looks down from its rocks upon wild deer and gazelles grazing unscared in the vicinity of the habitations of man.

II.

ITS HISTORY.

The Caucasus is celebrated as the scene of some of the most popular fables of Grecian antiquity, as well as of some of the earliest traditions of the race. For while the ark of Noah is said to have grounded on the top of Mount Elbrus before reaching its final resting-place on the neighboring Ararat, it was on Kasbek that Prometheus was chained to a rock for having stolen the fire of the gods and given it to mortals. In the mountain land of Colchis, Jason carried off the golden fleece, and Cadmus reaped a harvest of armed men from sowing serpent's teeth in furrows turned by the fire-breathing bulls of Vulcan. Hither wandered that primitive race of men who were driven by the Pelasgi from the regions of Olympus; on an island off the

1*

coast the poets located the palace of Aurora, wherein were kept up the perpetual dances and songs of the hours, and where was daily reborn the sun; and finally, between the present Little Kabarda and Svanethi existed, say the traditions, the gallant state of the Amazons, until the heart of their otherwise unconquerable prophetess was taken captive by Thoulme, chief of the Circassians, while long afterwards the famous Nina continued to rule over the heroic sisterhood in Immeritia.

The ancient Persians gave to the Caucasus the name of Seddi Iskender, or the barrier of Alexander, who here met with the first check in his attempt to subjugate the world. Rome early sent her conquering legions to bring under the yoke the prosperous colonies of Greece on the shores of the Euxine; and Pompey returning home from the East, after having chased Mithridates from the Euphrates to Colchis and Dioscurias, graced his triumphal entry into the city with the gigantic sons of these mountains. Genoa, in a later and more commercial age, made settlements on the Caucasian shore, whither she sent her argosies to be freighted with grain, skins, tallow, and the fruits of the hive, and where she has left to this day the foundations of her walls and towers, her carved stones and crosses, her sepulchres and a name. In more recent times, the princes of the dynasties of the White Horde and the Golden Camp have come from the Crimea to break their lances on the plains of the Kuma; Attila, Tamerlane, and Genghis Khan have swept in their victorious career along the base of these rocky ramparts of freedom; the Persian and the Turk have waged occasional war with some of the Caucasian tribes, though never with more than partial and temporary success; and it is the Muscovite empire alone which has ever succeeded in throwing the shadows of imminent subjugation over the landscape of these sunny vales.

Accordingly, the independence of most of these mountain tribes has been maintained from the earliest times to the present against all the attempts of their enemies of the plains. They have lived for generations, the memory of man runneth not to the end of, in the enjoyment of a large degree of natural liberty, in obedience to ancient laws and usages, in the respect of age, virtue, and superiority in arms, and now furnish the only specimen left of tribes of men still living in all the simplicity, and retaining, along with the practice of some of the semi-barbarous vices, all the heroism of the so-called age of gold.

Georgia, which lies on the southern declivities of the Caucasus, was nominally converted to Christianity in the days of Constantine the Great, when its heroic queen Thamar ruled over one of the most powerful empires of western Asia; but beautiful on these mountain tops as were the feet of those who brought the glad tidings and published peace, the doctrines of the cross made but little impression on the benighted minds of these worshippers in the temple of nature. Nor though Russia early endeavored to introduce the peaceful soldiers of the church into the fastnesses where she could not penetrate with her secular dragoons, the native heart continued to hold to the simple religious rites handed down by tradition from the fathers, and finally relinquished them only within the last hundred years in exchange for the doctrines of the Prophet, which, though introduced a couple of centuries before, at the point of the spears of the Crimean Khans, were then first made plain and acceptable by missionaries from Turkey.

For subsistence the Caucasian tribes have always relied mainly on pasturage and agriculture, also on the chase, on rapine and the spoils of war, and on the exchange of their natural products and slaves for the salt, gunpowder, and manufactured goods of foreigners. So constant for centuries has been their attachment to the mountains that they have never emigrated to the plains, the life of which they despise. Only the harems of Constantinople have an attraction for their females; and a few restless youth, wandering at different times into foreign parts, have furnished body-guards to the sultans of Turkey and the Khans of the Crimea; have served under the name of Mamelukes in Egypt, where Mehemet Ali could not control but only massacre them; and latterly have graced the parade days of the Russian capital, where, treated like pet lions, their fiery spirit of independence and impatience of discipline have been but mildly restrained by the Czar, and where such is their haughty, imposing bearing, that whenever the vulgar crowd in the streets gives way for the coming of any one, it has become almost a proverb to say, it is either a general officer in the army or a Circassian.

III.

THE WAR WITH RUSSIA.

The contest between the Circassians and the Russians may be said to have originated as far back as the middle ages. For it was in the tenth century that the grand duke Swätoslaff, overrunning a portion of the Bosphoric territories, came into collision with the inhabitants of the Caucasus; and in the sixteenth, the Russians under the grand duke Wassiljewitsch made their appearance on the Caspian, on the western coast of which they established garrisons as far south as Tarku. In the latter century also the Kabardian princes, whose territory consisting of open valleys was less defended by nature against the inroads of enemies, bowed their necks for a time in submission; and Georgia, on the

Asiatic slope, took in the person of her king Alexander the oath of vassalage to the Muscovite, obtaining a master where she had asked only for a protector. But occupied during the next two hundred years with affairs at the north, the Russian princes lost their possessions and most of their influence in the Caucasus; and it was not until 1722 that the far-seeing ambition of the great Peter brought him to the "Albanian gates" of Derbend, and even within sight of the sacred fires of the promontory of Apsheron.

It was permitted to this most gifted of the czars to behold these mountains and get a glimpse of the fair Asiatic vales beyond, but not to possess them. In leaving, however, to his successors the legacy of his boundless ambition, he pointed with his dying hand to the peaks of Elbrus and Kasbek; and ever since his race, extending itself on all sides, has not ceased to press onward in this pathway toward the rising of the sun.

Especially within the last quarter of a century has Russia occupied herself in earnest with the conquest of the Caucasus. During that period she has maintained there constantly a large force, and latterly as many as two hundred thousand men under arms. Year after year she has despatched her battalions to supply the places of those who had fallen by the shaskas of the Circassians or the still more deadly arrows of the fever, which in the most sickly seasons has cut off no less than one sixth of the whole army. She has sent thither also her best generals and administrators from Jermoloff to Paskiewitsch and Woronzoff. The emperor Nicholas went himself into these mountains at the risk of his life, to inspect and encourage by his presence the invading columns. Every system of attack which the ingenuity of the St. Petersburg cabinet could devise has in turn been tried; efforts have constantly been made to gain over by intrigue the tribes who could not be subjugated by force; the cross, joining its influence to the power of the sword, has endeavored to bring the native mind under the dominion of a system of religion more favorable to the aims of the autocrat; a superior civilization has held out to the comparatively rude barbarians, its hands full of gifts dazzling and fatal to liberty; but hitherto mostly, if not all, in vain. The inhabitants of the upper and more inaccessible mountains have held their independence above all price, fighting for their homes as the mountaineer only will; and the chieftains who have been tempted by preferment in the Russian army and the glitter of its epaulettes, by the honors of the parades at Tiflis, and even by the imperial champaign, and the sight of the ballet dancers of St. Petersburg, have disdained to sell a birthright of freedom inherited from a thousand generations in exchange for these high-flavored sops of an overreaching foreign despotism.

An intense interest of humanity, therefore, still hangs over this prolonged contest between the forces of civilization and those of the primitive state of nature, between the battalions of imperial authority and the bands of democratic liberty; and the more intense because this barrier of nature and wall of freemen once completely carried, there will remain no further hinderance to the victorious course eastward of that ambition which, possessing already the path to the orient by the northern snows, covets that also across the sands of the tropics.

IV.

HIS BIRTHPLACE.

SCHAMYL, the principal hero of this war of independence, was born in the year 1797. The place of his birth is Himri, an aoul or village in the district of Arrakan, and in the north-western part of Daghestan, a territory lying on the Caspian. It is situated on the river, called lower down where it approaches the sea, the Sulak, but here the Koissu; and at a point just above where the main stream throws off that one of its four branches which is termed the Andian Koissu.

All these waters flow down, on the south, from the main Caucasian range; on the west, from the Andian offshoot; and on the east, from that of the Kaitach; which two latter running, the one north-easterly and the other north-westerly until they meet, form the two sides of a triangle of mountains having for its base the high Caucasus. The apex is just below Himri, and consists of the escaped cliffs of two summits called the Touss-Tau and the Sala-Tau; while through a gorge between them is precipitated the whole volume of the united branches of the Koissu. Himri, accordingly, together with the neighboring fortified aoul of Akhulgo, is one of the keys of this triangular region of well-watered highlands, which is inhabited by a considerable number of warlike tribes known collectively as the Lesghians, and which, with the territory of Daghestan on the east, and that of Tchetchenia on the north, is the principal theatre of the great military achievements of Schamyl.

The aoul of Himri is placed like an eagle's nest high on a rock projecting from the mountain side. From the beautiful vale through which winds the Koissu, a narrow path cut out of the rock is carried zig-zag up a height of two or three hundred feet, and is exposed to be swept by stones let loose from above of any enemy that might be daring enough to attack this strong-hold. A triple wall supported by high towers adds the defences of art to those of nature; while above, the place is sheltered by the overhanging brow of the mountain.

Standing on one of these towers the native looks down upon the narrow but fertile valley, divided in twain by the fast-flowing river. Several of the surrounding mountains are laid out in terraced gardens; while some are partially covered with oaks and plane-trees; and others again are entirely bare, having instead of the drapery of foliage only the tints of gold or purple which the rising and the setting sun sheds over the ruggedness of the limestone and the porphyry. Near at hand are seen one or two heights which are clad with perpetual snows; while westward, far away beyond the lower highlands, the view is terminated by the white form of Mt. Kasbek.

The internal aspect of the aoul is less pleasing. Most of the streets are steep and crooked, though the scattered position of the dwellings in others, affords some sites both open and level. The roofs are generally flat; the walls, almost destitute of windows, are rough with unhewn stones; and many of the houses lie half buried under the rocky mountain side. These are without numbers as the streets are without names. Here, moreover, rises no village spire to point the thoughts of men heavenward; no church bell rings out its merry festal peals, or tolls the march to the grave; no sundial marks the succession of the hours which pass by unheeded all, save those of morning, noon, and evening; and in no public school-house is heard the low buzz of children conning their tasks. But the mollah calls to prayers from the minaret of a humble mosque; and in a dark corner illumined by aslant rays from a small high window in a wall, teaches to some half a dozen urchins the strange Arabic letters and the chants of the Koran. From the going down of the sun until early morn not a light is seen throughout the aoul, nor scarcely a sound heard, save the howling of the watch-dogs and the plaintive crying of the jackals in the forests. Indeed, the only hour in the day when there is any appearance of life in these streets is at noon, when the labors of the garden and the exercises of the games being suspended, many of the male inhabitants either sit about idle, or lie sleeping like Italian lazzaroni, or stand grouped together in long, light-colored surtouts with a negligent grace and natural dignity not surpassed in antique statues. Here and there one more diligent burnishes his arms, and another grooms his horse. A few veiled women come and go, bearing jars of water or other burdens, though most of the female population are occupied in their apartments with the preparation of food, and in the labors of the loom and spindle; while young children, half-naked, play around the house doors and through the lanes with an activity in strong contrast with the prevailing tone of grave and somnolent repose.

V.

HIS PARENTS, ATALIK, AND TEACHER.

Of the parents of Schamyl nothing is known; nor is this lack of information greatly to be regretted, considering that they lived in a state of society where there is so little inequality of classes or diversity of external condition. His father not being probably a chief of the tribe, was a freeman and peer among his fellows, possessing like them a small, amphitheatrical house, the husband of but one wife, owning a war-horse, and arms, besides a few sheep and goats, and the proprietor of a garden supported by terraces on a neighboring mountain side.

Nor is it known who was his foster-father, or atalik; for according to the custom prevalent in western, and to some extent in eastern

Circassia, he may at an early age have been adopted by some one in whose family he resided during the years spent in learning the rudiments of letters and the art of war, and who sustained a relation towards him even more intimate and affectionate than that of his own father. The atalik would have supplied the boy with food and clothing, instruction, and a home, without expecting any other compensation than such plunder as the latter during his pupilage might bring in from the enemy, together with the gratitude through life of both himself and his family. And this he could well afford to do, being possessed of means somewhat superior to those of the majority of his clansmen. If descended from a family among the first in the tribe and long illustrious in arms, he might own as many as fifteen hundred head of cattle, and an equal number of sheep, besides a small herd of horses and mares. Like the ancient patriarchs, he would have his wives and his servants, some of them captured in forays, and all living together as one family in a stone house of several stories and defended by a high tower.

This practice of transferring young children from the parental mansion to that of an atalik, seems to have had its origin in the same fear lest natural affection might lead to effeminacy of character which induced the Spartans to send their infants on a shield to be delivered over to the nursery of the State. In accordance with a similar custom, also, was the young Achilles intrusted by Peleus to the care of Chiron, the centaur. For among the Circassians, as among the early Greeks, the principal object of education is to form the accomplished warrior.

History has been fortunate enough, however, to get possession of the name of Schamyl's instructor, who is called Dschelal Eddin, and who, beginning the education of the future prophet by teaching him the Arabic language, completed it by initiating him into the doctrines of the Sufis. He still lives, a venerable man, and is said to be the only person to whom his pupil in after-life ever granted his entire confidence, and at whose feet he has been known ever to sit for counsel.

The learning of letters, however, was not

the boy's first lesson in that course of training which prepared him to become a leader of the tribes; for as in the history of the race, so in the education of the warrior in these mountains, the practice of horsemanship comes before the study of books.

VI.

HIS EARLY EDUCATION.

In the due course of Circassian education Schamyl could not have been four years old when he exchanged the amusement of building houses of mud and pebble-stones for that of backing horses. A couple of years later his atalik might even have presented him with a steed for the practice of those arts of horsemanship wherein the Circassians excel the most expert riders in the world. The Koissu must also have submitted to the triumph of his arms when their bone was still in the gristle, and during the warm season of the year have suffered, both at morning and evening, its torrent to be breasted by the daring young swimmer. To wrestle, the boy, without doubt, began almost as soon as he was able to stand alone; and to dance was learned without a master, whether according to the figures practised in the ring of pleasure, or the more active steps taken in the pantomimic fight. Shooting with the bow, the gun, and the pistol, is an exercise for Circassian boys at an age when those of countries more civilized are spelling, syllable by syllable, the lessons of the primer and the catechism. The art of thieving adroitly is also reckoned an accomplishment by these mountaineers, as formerly by the Spartans, when the despoiled is an enemy, or at least a member of another tribe. And as in their council-rings there is as often an opportunity for the display of eloquence as ever there was before the walls of ancient Troy, so the youth are taught both by observation and by direct lessons the art of persuasion.

In early childhood Schamyl is said to have enjoyed a somewhat less rugged health than his mates; and had the development of his mind been forced by the training to which the children of civilization are generally subjected, being compelled to sit by the hour upon a bench and breathe the unwholesome air of an over-heated school-room, very likely after having passed, during a brief season, for a youthful prodigy in the eyes of an admiring, but inconsiderate circle of friends, he would have closed his earthly career and been lamented as a genius for this world too brilliant and too good. But in this comparative state of barbarism, the boy's mind having been allowed more slowly and naturally to unfold itself, and his body meanwhile being strengthened by a life in the open air of the mountains, and by such athletic sports as well supplied the place of the games of the ancient Greeks and Romans, this fine spirit was saved from premature decay, to the honor of his country, and the illustration of humanity.

Nor could it have been long before these arts, all more or less having reference to the formation of the skilful warrior, were put to the test of practice in actual service. There are reliable accounts of Circassian boys who at the age of ten years have gone to the wars, as unable to eat or sleep on the approach of the enemy as in occidental countries are the rustic lads on the eve of a muster of the county militia, at which in addition to the show of red-coats and cocked hats there will be cakes, pop-beer, tumbling, and monkeys. Many a young mountaineer before he has got a beard has "bagged his five Russians." At first, indeed, the boy is allowed only, it may be, to pass the night with the sentinels on the hills, or to watch the horses of the sleeping warriors, and afterwards sees his first battle-field, going out on an expedition in the quality of page of some chieftain, taking charge of his steed when he alights, and attending upon his person.

In this preparatory training and the practice of these athletic sports the boy Schamyl must have passed the first dozen years of his life, living in the house of his atalik, and very rarely visiting that of his father. Nor even when he did so was it to sit, much less to eat in the paternal presence, but only with his back reverently turned and his head stuck in a corner.

But at the end of this period of discipline, having become more than a tyro, if not already an expert in all manly exercises and warlike arts, the lad must have been restored to his parents by his foster-father. The event is always celebrated by a feast at which all the relatives of the two families are invited, and from which the atalik returns loaded with presents, and with thanks. It is indeed a proud day for the youngster, because it is his putting on of the toga. Thenceforward, if not fully a man, he is at least a mad-cap or *deli-kan.*

VII.

HIS HORSEMANSHIP.

Schamyl, now become a *deli-kan,* is said to have been so ambitious of the palm in all youthful games that whenever defeated he would brood for days together over his disgrace in silent chagrin. From his childhood he knew not how to brook a superior.

He therefore zealously continued his exercises, particularly those in horsemanship. Like that of all Circassian youth it was his ambition not only to sit his horse a perfect centaur, to dash at full speed up steeps and down precipices, to leap the chasm and to swim the torrent; but also on the gallop to discharge his weapons, in an instant unslinging his gun from behind his back, and as

3*

quickly returning it to its place; to hang suspended from the side of the horse so as to avoid the aim of an enemy; to spring to the ground for the purpose of picking up something and again vault into the saddle without halting; and to take aim with such precision as to hit the smallest and most inconveniently placed mark while going at full tilt.

The subduing of a half-wild horse in the herd which is allowed during a portion of the year to roam the woods and hills, is also a feat frequently practised by the Circassian cavalier, either for the sake of securing the animal, or simply as an exercise in horsemanship. A rider or two armed with lassos plunge into the midst of the herd, and selecting one of the wildest of the stallions — for mares are not used under the saddle — secure him by throwing over his head the noose. Then the cavalier who is to make trial of his skill springs upon the back of the animal, which with dilated eyes and smoking nostrils exhibits the greatest consternation. And now commences the contest between horse and rider. Furious as well as frightened the brute speeds like an arrow over the hills or down the valleys. He turns and doubles, halts suddenly, rolls on the ground, crawls on his belly, dashes into the midst of the herd, and tries in all possible ways to get rid of the burden he has no fancy for. But the intrepid rider, self-possessed, and constantly on the alert, sits upon his back as if a part of the animal, waving his hand in triumph after every struggle terminated in his favor; and there he continues to sit and hold the mastery until the strong steed, finally exhausted by his efforts, covered with foam, out of breath, and cowed in spirit, acknowledges the superiority of his antagonist.

When tamed, however, the Circassian horse is both perfectly gentle and attached to his master. The pet brought up in the yard is as playful as a kitten. The children gambol with him. His master fondles him, patting his neck and kissing his head. On festal days and occasions of ceremony he is decked out with red-cloth trappings; his neck is wreathed with many-colored glass beads; ribands are tied in his mane; and bunches of wild flowers nod from his foretop. The stranger may not praise the Circassian's wife or child for fear of shedding over them the malign influence of the evil eye, or for other reasons less fanciful; but to the praises of his steed the warrior's ear is ever open. The faithful animal is his companion on all his excursions; he drinks with him the waters which flow through the plains of the enemy; he looks down as well as himself from the rock on the passing column and the squares of infantry; he shares with him the dangers of the bayonet and the bullet; and, neighing, participates too in the hurrah of the onset and the shouts of victory. Trained to take part in the ambuscade, he will creep after his master like a dog, and lie crouching at his feet in silence. No unkind word is ever spoken to him; nor is he ever beaten; so that his spirit is unbroken, and his attachment to his lord is manifested by the pleasure he takes in his caresses, the gladness with which, snorting and pawing the ground, he receives him on his back, the pride of step and eye with which he bears him off, the fury with which he dashes into the fight and pursues the enemy, and the intelligent fidelity with which he obeys every movement of the rein or the hand, dutiful until he falls bleeding at last on the field of battle, or at a very advanced age is relieved from further service, and with clipt tail and mane is turned out to graze the peaceful pastures until the day of his death.

There are a number of varieties of the Circassian horse, though without very marked differences. Those of Kabarda are among the most famed; and excellent cavalry horses are got by Pratof's stallions out of the Tartar and Kalmuck mares. These are valued at from two to three hundred roubles. The Turcoman breed also is highly esteemed, standing about fifteen hands high, in perfect training, and joining to the strength of a bull the spirit of a lion. But universally throughout the Caucasus the native horse is docile, fleet, capable of enduring very great fatigue, of supporting very great privations, possessed of the most undeniable mettle, and endowed with the largest measure of intelligence and affection within the capacity of the animal's nature. In the best breeds his pedigree is kept with care; and the mark of his master is branded in the shape of a horse-shoe, an arrow, or some similar device on his haunches.

VIII.

THE CIRCASSIAN GAMES.

THROWING the djerrid was perhaps the delikan's favorite equestrian amusement. To play this game a certain number of combatants, belonging often to two different aouls or districts, assemble at an appointed place, each mounted on his steed, and armed with a long white wand or staff. At a given signal they all set off at full gallop in pursuit of each other, the object of the race being to give blows and avoid receiving them. The staves accordingly are seen flying through the air in all directions. The dexterity with which the combatants manage to elude each other's blows, catch a stave thrown at them, pick up one from the ground, and that without alighting or losing a moment's time, is to the stranger who for the first time beholds the sport truly astonishing. When a horseman who happens to be without a djerrid gets entangled among his opponents, he will be seen twisting and turning with the activity of a wild-cat in order to elude the blows aimed at him; now completely screened under the belly of the horse, then lying at full length on his back, and again stretched by his side, until regaining a djerrid he becomes in turn the assailant. In this rough sport only the greatest agility and suppleness of limbs, combined with extraordinary physical strength, can secure the palm, while the less dexterous combatants may not escape without the disgrace of broken heads.

Another feat which only long practice will enable the young rider to perform, is one of archery. A mark is attached to the top of several lofty poles fastened together so as to elevate it to a considerable height. Then a horseman starting a short distance from the pole rides towards it at full speed, and just before reaching it, suddenly bends his bow, stoops to the left side of his horse the instant before the latter passes to the right of the pole, and then twisting himself around with his face turned back and looking almost directly upwards, lets fly the shaft perpendicularly. The difficulty of the position, joined to the speed of the horse, renders the hitting of the mark a proof of the highest skill; and even where the competition is spirited, the victors are few.

Running for the flag is a game in which the fleetness and bottom of the horse are tested perhaps more than the expertness of the rider. A number of cavaliers having assembled, one of them taking a small flag, or crimson scarf, or pistol cover embroidered by the fair hands of the belle of the aoul, starts off on the gallop, his prize streaming in the wind like a meteor. The others, after having given him the advantage in the start, pursue for the purpose of overtaking him; for whoever succeeds in coming up with the flag-bearer takes his place, and so to the end of the race. With grace and impetuosity they dash down the valley, over the hills, and along the mountain side. The flag-bearer aims to keep the lead not only by quick running but also by turning and doubling, by taking advantage of the ground and placing obstacles between himself and his pursuers. To the right, to the left, straightforward, over brooks and fences, across torrent and ravine, through woods and thickets, up hill and down dale, away sweeps the mad cavalcade. 'T is neck or nothing, and leaps that only dares the devil. Overtaken, the bearer of the flag yields it up to his successful competitor, who shouting his triumphant *vo-ri-ra-ka* hurries onwards with the whole legion at his heels. So they race until the hardy horses, though eager as their riders for the victory, are obliged at last to halt for breath. But after an interval of rest, starting with another hurrah the troop go over the course again, and perhaps again, until the contest is ended, and some fortunate deli-kan is pronounced entitled to the prize.

It is a common occurrence during these games for a mounted horseman when particularly excited to throw up his cap; and this is always regarded as a challenge by any of his companions, unslinging, uncovering, and cocking his gun, to put a ball through it before it reaches the ground. Or a bonnet is purposely dropped, that some rider going at full speed may display his agility by picking it up without drawing rein. Again, there is the game in which two mounted cavaliers set off at full speed holding each other by the hand, and each endeavoring by main strength or dexterity to pull his antagonist from the saddle. And finally, a party of horsemen on arriving at a friendly aoul or place of general gathering, is met by a company of persons on foot who, bearing branches of trees, make a dash at the horses' heads in order if possible to frighten them. This tests the skill of the riders, and also trains the horses to rush without fear upon the enemy.

IX.

HIS LOVE OF NATURE.

SCHAMYL in early youth exhibited a remarkable sensibility to the beauty and sublimity of nature. It is related of him by the aged men of Himri that he was fond of climbing the neighboring mountains, and that especially at the going down of the sun he might be seen sitting on a high point of rock whence he could survey at the same time the vale below and the fantastic summits which tower above it. There he would sit gazing at the snows red with the declining rays, and at the rocks glowing in the reflected purple of the clouds, until the valley and the glens connected with it were quite dark with the gathering twilight — gazing where far off to the westward the snow-clad peaks were still burning brightly as with altar fires that reached to heaven—gazing where blazed longest of all the top of Kasbek, until from its expiring spark the evening planet seemed to catch the light with which it flamed out in the sky above it, while gradually the lower mountains faded on the sight, and only the heavens and the highest peaks were bathed in the mild light of night.

This moreover was enchanted ground. For on one side of the loftiest and most grotesque of the heights around Himri, there leans against it a level table rock of considerable extent which is perfectly desolate, and which the superstitious imaginations of the inhabitants of this aoul have made the scene of almost as much witchery as was ever located on the top of the Brocken. Often in the dead of night, say the villagers, strange fires are lighted on this dancing floor of the spirits, and which reflect on all the mountain sides a lurid and unearthly glare. Then the great white eagle which for a thousand years has housed in the high Caucasus hastens hither on wings which shake the air like the sighing of the night wind, or the howling of the coming tempest; and then assemble here from fairy land the happy peris, who in this lighted chamber dance on fantastic toes until the day peeps over the mountain tops or the first cock crows in Himri.

But while no one dared to tread this haunted rock after the going down of the sun, it was precisely here that Schamyl, whose intellect, self-illumined, early pierced through the blind which superstition binds over the eyes of all mountaineers, often selected his seat and lingered through the twilight far into the darkness of the evening. With his trustful love of nature he feared no supernatural powers; and while the common mind was filled with dread in the presence of phenomena which, real or imaginary, it could not explain, he found therein only such subjects for reflection as fascinated his imagination and filled his soul with devout admiration of the creative spirit which pervades all things.

Once, some of his companions offended by some high, scornful words of his, let drop in the excitement of the games, resolved to waylay and maltreat him on his return from the heights in the edge of the evening. They accordingly set upon the enthusiast as descending from the mountain tops his thoughts still lingered behind, but who quickly recovering his presence of mind stood on the defensive. Numbers, however, overpowered him ; and he fell bleeding from wounds on his head, arm, and body. But being still able to regain his home, though faint with the loss of blood, he bound up his wounds himself, and with the assistance of a doctoress skilled in simples, made such applications of herbs as at the end of several weeks restored him to health again. Ashamed, however, to acknowledge that he had been beaten even when the odds were greatly against him, he said not a word respecting his illness to any one, save to his revered teacher Dschelal Eddin, to whom he confidentially made known the circumstances of the encounter.

X.

HUNTING.

SCHAMYL'S love for exploring the mountains would naturally make him fond of hunting, as are his countrymen generally, when not occupied with the higher game of war.

The larger kinds of game being abundant in these mountains, and the use of small shot being unknown, bird-shooting is but little practised, and the fowl fly in these heavens as unscared as in the original paradise. The nightingale sings in the thickets; the woodpecker makes the primeval woods resound with his chisel; crows of the pink and black species croak from the dead branches of the oaks; ravens with dark red legs and scarlet bills build their nests in the top of the elms; detachments of blue wood-pigeons cover the fields as numerous and as tame as sparrows; mergansers and golden-eyed ducks haunt in numerous flocks the running waters; and wild geese flying down in the month of December from the Russian wastes, halt on their way to the waters of Persia, and mixed with swans, float in stately fleets on the shores of both the Euxine and the Caspian. The falcon hawk also is constantly circling over the hills and swooping down into the valleys; the eagle may be seen soaring above his eyrie on Elbrus or Kasbek; the rapacious vulture watches from the high overhanging points of rock the lower woods and pastures; the melancholy owl hoots through the night around the hamlets; and by the side of the lowly mountain tarn stands silent and solitary the pelican of the wilderness. Only the wild turkey in the pinetree's top is a mark for the rifle; or the pheasant, darting up out of the path into the overhanging branches, tempts occasionally the sharpshooter; while, on the contrary, woodcock and snipe bore for worms in every marsh and mud-bank, undisturbed by setter or by pointer.

The wild boar hunt is the chief sport in Circassian venery. This animal frequents the banks of the rivers overgrown with reeds, and the ravines of the mountains filled with thickets. Both the valleys and the marshes adjacent are ploughed by his snout; nor is the farmer's stock-yard entirely secure from the crunching of his tusks. He is hunted with dogs, generally resembling a cross between the greyhound and the colley of the Scottish highlands. When found the furious beast will sometimes stand at bay, ripping up and tossing in the air a pack of enemies; but generally with horrid gruntings and snortings he plunges down the ravine or canters over the marsh, big almost as a Highland cow, driving aside the tall reeds or saplings as if simple spears of grass, a black monster, bristled, with projecting tusks, and eyes bloodshot. But the well-directed rifle ball pierces at last his tough flanks; the enormous mass reeling rolls over in the mire; and the unclean carcass is left to be feasted on by vultures and prowling wolves.

There are elk on the Kuban; but the following of the fallow deer in the hills is more common. The hunter searches for the beds of the roes with dogs, or stalking the forests steals upon the herd when browsing upon the tender twigs and the moss of trees, or cropping the herbs along the skirts of the pastures. There are several varieties of them, but all tolerably wild from being so much pursued in the chase; though the sight of this graceful animal is common enough in the farm-yards, where it has been tamed, and where when young it is a great pet.

A fine breed of greyhounds is kept for coursing the hares. These abound, burrowing in all the mountains, and everywhere nibbling with their sharp teeth the herbage. After a slight fall of snow they are easily tracked; and rarely does the hunter, on awaking in the morning, find the earth newly clad with this white mantle that he does not call his hounds and set off for the fields. The keen air of the morning late in autumn invites to active exercise as the rising sun pours its crimson flood over the hills, all changed in a single night by the witchery of the noiselessly fallen flakes. The dogs eye alternately the hills and their master as they run; and the hunter with overflowing spirits and every nerve drawn tight enters rejoicing into the race.

XI.

CAMPING OUT.

Occasionally in the autumnal months a party of huntsmen is made up for an excursion into the high Caucasus. Such expeditions constitute a memorable event in the life of the deli-kan; and it may well be believed that Schamyl must have embraced the opportunity thereby offered of beholding the grandeur of nature amidst "the thousand peaks."

There would be but little need of preparation. For the Circassian wears his cartouche pockets constantly on his breast; any extra ammunition, together with a scanty supply of provisions, is easily attached to the saddle-bow; the steed is always ready for service; the dogs are eager to set off; and so at short notice the whole party gallops out of the aoul with hurrahs and pistol-firing.

On the journey, however, they ride slowly. For the road is but a path in the mountains, narrow and rugged, often steep of ascent and descent, for the most part following by the side of the watercourses, and in the dry beds of the torrents, or winding around the mountain sides, by the edge of precipices, and across chasms bridged only by the leap. Indeed so great are the difficulties of the way that the rider is very often obliged to dismount and allow his horse to follow after him as best he can.

At mid-day they halt for a couple of hours for luncheon; and with the going down of the sun they pitch their tent for the night. For this purpose an opening in the forest beside a spring of water, or the bank of a running stream is selected, where the horses, relieved of their saddles, may find pasture. At morning and noon a little flour of millet and honey suffices for the meals. This in fact is the usual war-provision, and is said to be a diet which gives strength to both body and mind. Being carried in a skin hung at the saddle-bow it soon ferments, but is eaten afterwards with great relish, and may be kept in this condition for a considerable length of time. A cup to convey the water from the spring is made of the burdock leaf, which also answers the purpose of a carpet for the saying of prayers, and even furnishes afterward a grateful repast for the horses. To this frugal fare, however, will very likely be added at evening a pheasant or hare, a turkey or a deer shot on the road, and cooked either by being roasted before the fire, or laid, cut in slices, on live embers. Whatever chance game the luck of the day may furnish for the supper, it will be sure to be eaten with a relish that will need no sauce; though even with nothing more than his unleavened bread and water the Circassian is perfectly contented, and adds thanks therefor in his prayers.

Supper finished, ablutions performed, and prayers said, the hunters unroll their blankets, placing one on the ground and the other over them, with their feet turned towards the fire blazing with large logs of wood; and so under the protection of the open heavens and the stars, which are the thousand watchful eyes of Allah, his simple children sleep.

In entering upon the region of the higher mountains the valleys grow narrower, showing only here and there a mere line of green, or oftener, the silver thread of torrents rushing headlong over the rocks. Strong was the contrast when in an opening between the mountains the hunter looked down upon the shepherd's cottage, with its shade of nut-bearing trees and its fold of white fleeces, or upon a patch of cultivated ground high among the rocks to which the husbandman climbs for the sake of a few handfuls of grain, or the pasture of his cow or goat; and when, on the other hand, he beheld around him, as was often the case, only the mountain tops sparsely covered with dwarfed oaks and plane-trees, the rocks frequently naked save here and there the covering of moss, the immense masses broken up into clefts and chasms, piled on top of each other in forms the most shapeless and grotesque, an utter waste, and the more desolate from some wild bird of the mountains which occasionally flapped its wings overhead, or the wild goat which startled sprang away among the distant rocks.

Yet there are localities still higher up

where from favorable exposure the mountaineer pushes an adventurous plough, tilling his slope with rifle slung at his back, and gathering his harvest full three months later than in the plains below. Here, too, blooms the Caucasian rose or rhododendron, and the azalia-pontica, from the blossoms of which is made the honey of that intoxicating quality mentioned by Strabo, and which, when mixed in small quantity with the ordinary mead, forms a beverage as potent as the alcoholic liquors of the north.

On reaching the snow-line of the Kasbek, at farthest, the progress of the hunters would be arrested. On their way hither they would have occasionally brought down a fallow deer or a fat bear, besides pheasants and the wild hens of the mountains, hares, and large grey squirrels. They might even have had a shot or two at a wild sheep or buffalo, which as well as horses sometimes roam untamed the mountains; and from time to time their rifles must have been tempted also by the porcupine crossing their path, by the fox surprised far from his hole, by the wild-cat driven into a tree, and even by the wolf prowling around their steps towards nightfall.

Here, with the never-melting snows not far overhead, they would find small stone houses erected expressly for the use of the chamois-hunter. For along these elevated crags runs and bounds the nimble rupicapra; in certain favorite tracts is occasionally met the ibex, roaming solitary over his scanty pastures; and on the very highest rocks, where in winter they lie with faces to the wind, insensible to the most intense cold, are seen herds of still another species of the wild goat resembling in shape the tamed one, but larger, having long beautiful horns, and flesh with the dainty flavor of venison.

XII.

IN THE WHITE MOUNTAINS.

But proud as is the returning hunter of the beautiful chamois horns hung upon his saddle-bow, it could scarcely be otherwise than that the soul of one so smitten with the love of natural scenery as was Schamyl, should here be more occupied with contemplating the grandeur of the mountain tops than in chasing the timid, graceful animals which thereupon find a home. If in the course of his ascent he had kept his eyes pretty steadily fixed upon the magnificent summits far off white with snows, but nearer blue with the ice which has led the Tartars to give to them the name of Ialbus or ice-mane; if lower down he had gazed with admiration at the oaks which for two centuries had grasped with their roots and overspread with their branches the rocks in situations to which upon the Alps and the Pyrenees only climbs the pine; and if higher up he had not passed by unnoticed even the lowly pink and rose of the mountains, blooming along the snow-line, but even there sought out by the bee and the butterfly of Apollo; how would he be overwhelmed with the sublimity of the scene on finding himself in the dread company of Kasbek and the hundred other peaks which are his vassals! Standing on the steps of the throne of this, like Elbrus, dsching padischah, or king of spirits, he would gaze around upon a host of cones and needles glittering in the sunlight, while far below lay the Black or wooded mountains, looking for the most part with the same face of precipices upon the remoter steppes as do the White mountains on themselves. Indeed there is wanting only the lakes of the Bernese Alps, glaciers as magnificent as those of Chamouni, and cascades like the Staubbach and the fall of the Aar to make this Caucasian range the most beautiful, as it probably is the most sublime, on the face of the earth.

Still the Caucasus boasts of more majestic woods and a more luxuriant flora than the Alps; and when to its scenery is added the coloring lent it by the rising and the setting sun, there can be no higher beauty in nature anywhere. Especially during the summer months travellers have noted a remarkable purity of atmosphere in these mountains, and represent them as being full of light a considerable time before the appearing of the sun on the horizon; while in autumn there is sufficient vapor to furnish the landscape with that drapery of blue mist and variously tinted clouds, so characteristic of the summer views of the Alps. In this long interval, between the break of day and the complete sunrise, it seems to the dullest observer as if nature were standing wrapt in adoration of the great Creator. Clad in snows and ice the thousand peaks are like white-robed priests ministering in a temple not made with hands; and when the loftiest tops are tipped with the purple of the coming day, it is as it were the incense-burning censers which they swing high in heaven. Then the lower mountains, too, receive an additional beauty when the level rays light up with a still brighter red the mighty masses of porphyry, and the dark granite glows with a vermilion not its own. Every variety and form of rock is transfigured by the new-born light from heaven. The white chalkstone glitters from afar; the light grey feldspar assumes a warm flesh tint; the limestone becomes straw color; the crystals of hornblende flash like fire-flies; and the veins of white quartz, running with their nodules of serpentine and chlorite through the dark clay-slate, gleam as do chain lightnings through the clouds.

At sight of the gathering tempest the superstitious huntsman is not entirely exempt from terror. Some of the calcareous mountains, like the Beschtau, for example, being a perfect barometer, he knows, when their top becomes covered with clouds as with a hat, and their entire form is gradually enveloped in a mantle of mists, that there will be foul weather. Even the degree of wind and rain may be calculated with a considerable degree of certainty from the extent and different tints of the vapors; and if the indications are exceedingly threatening the hunter immediately erects his tent, if he have one, as on the ocean the sailor furls his canvas; or, lacking this protection, he seeks for the shelter of some projecting rock, or the entrance of a cavern. There when the sun is shrouded in clouds, and the blackness almost of night falls like a pall over the mountains, when the wind howls around the summits, and the thunder with its infinity of reverberations rattles, and bounds from crag to crag throughout the chain, seeming to make the very rocks tremble and totter, then affrighted he hears in the winds the flapping of the wings of that monstrous bird of the mountains whose age is a thousand years; in the lightnings which play over the abyss he sees the glaring eyes and waving mane of the wild white horse who, issuing from his stall under the glaciers, races with the storm; and in the thunders hears the resounding wheels of the chariot of Elijah kept, say some of the ancient Christian traditions, in the Redeemer's palace on the top of Kasbek.

But in a brief hour the storm is overpast;

for the changes of weather in this range of mountains, extending from one great sea to another, are sudden in all seasons of the year excepting summer. The clouds are rapidly rolled away to the eastward where the bow of promise spans the heavens as brilliant as when it was first bent over the neighboring Ararat, and where the accumulated piles of vapor are gorgeously burnished by the rays of the descending sun. Then rises over the broken ridge of the Black mountains the moon, just beginning, perhaps, to wane. How black indeed are they compared with the snow-white peaks which stand bathed in the silvery light. How black, too, is the abyss out of which rise the perpendicular cliffs, and the lofty conical shafts glittering with ice. The summits cast their long, sharply cut shadows athwart each other; every leaf on tree or plant which still holds its raindrop flashes as with a diamond; the night has not a breath of air; and nature lies entranced without a pulsation, save in the roar and trickling of everywhere falling waters.

XIII.

SONGS

It has been reported respecting the boy Schamyl that his parents being poor peasants he gained a livelihood by singing in the streets. But while this, not comporting well with Circassian manners and modes of life, is hardly to be credited, it is very probable that he began at an early age to sing the simpler popular airs, and might even when no more than four years old have amused his elders with his childish rendering of ballads above his comprehension. For the voice of song is often heard in these mountains; and, as in the days of Orpheus, the lyre still moves the rock of the Caucasian heart, taming with its gentle influences its wildness, and softening its asperity.

It is in songs that the Circassians, having no written language, have treasured up what little they possess of history; and by the constant singing of them have the traditions and myths of a very remote antiquity been handed down from generation to generation.

The wandering minstrel is the principal schoolmaster in the Caucasus. Wherever he arrives there is a friendly dispute in the hamlets as to who shall have the honor of rendering him the cup of hospitality. Every house in the aoul is open to receive him; he has always the best of entertainment; and his place in the social scale is, by general consent, fixed among the highest. He rehearses not only the legendary ballads to the listening circle of men and children, but conveys in song from tribe to tribe the chronicle of recent events, and the latest intelligence of the doings of the common enemy. His numbers describe how in some late foray the warriors, leaping down from the rocks, scattered the flax-haired Muscovites, and pillaged the stanitzas of the Cossacks. He wails the lament of the hero fallen in the battle field. He brands the coward and the traitor. He extols the green vales and strong rocks of the father-land; fans in every breast the love of independence; and celebrates in tenderer notes the praises of the fair.

His instrument is a kind of lyre not unlike our violin. It has but three strings which are made of horse-hair; the bow is almost an arc; and the head of the instrument rests, like that of the violoncello, on the ground or the divan.

Or the minstrel may accompany his strains upon the pipe, as is often done in the open air. Made of metal, even of silver, this instrument is one of considerable value; though more frequently it is a mere reed from the marshes of the Terek or the Kuban. It is usually about two feet in length; has three holes for the fingers near its lower extremity, and a short mouth-piece open at the sides. With something of the monotony of the bagpipe its notes are shrill; and when on the march among the hills the war-song is executed upon it, sometimes accompanied by the lyre, no "gathering" played to the pibroch ever more stirred the mountaineer heart in the highlands of Scotland.

The Circassians also beguile the way on their journeys with riding songs. These are sung in alternate strains, one being generally a clamorous recitative, and the other a kind of choral fugue, strange and romantic, and heard with pleasing effect in the mountains. Often when toiling at a foot-pace up the precipitous path of the torrent, or descending equally slow into the pass gloomy with impending rocks and drooping boughs, the travellers will burst involuntarily into a wild and plaintive lament over some fallen chieftain, one portion of the party singing in subdued tones a hurried chant like the English litany, and the other answering at the end of the stanzas with their full, mellow Ay! ay! a-ri-ra! which, like the pealing organ through the aisles, swells and floats away between the rocky sides of the glen.

Similar are the boat-songs on the Euxine and the Caspian. Of these there is a great variety, and all are chanted to the measured movement of the oars, now stronger, now weaker, and each stanza followed by a chorus.

Their A-ri-ra-cha always produces great effect on the rowers, and is mingled more or less with shouts, screams, and a mad-like laughter, while the long flat-bottomed canoe flies through the water driven by bending oars.

All festal occasions in Circassian life are enlivened by the presence of the minstrel. He is present when the warriors of the tribe assemble to sit in the council ring beneath the oaks; and in the intervals between the harangues of the orators who, sword in hand, urge the storming of a Russian fort or a raid upon the steppes, he fans the flame in their breasts by striking his lyre in praise of some hero illustrious in arms. When also a chieftain, desirous of raising a band of volunteers for some expedition against the enemy, rides from aoul to aoul summoning all good swords to follow, he transports along with him on the crupper of an attendant the aged minstrel, who at the gates sings the call to arms. His sightless eyeballs in frenzy roll, and the braves, both old and young, carried away now by his pathos and now by his rage, shout in chorus their ka-ri-ra, and spring into their saddles. And when at last, the warrior's race finished, his companions bring him, lashed on his steed, back at night to the aoul from which he rode so gayly forth in the morning, and with arms locked around each other's necks stand encircling the bard, the latter commences a monotonous but beautifully plaintive wail, his voice subdued with sorrow, and running at the end of the lines upon the same note, which rapidly caught and prolonged is like an uncontrollable gust of anguish, until the brothers in arms, no less impassioned, break in with a chorus so sad, slow, and low that every eye would fill with tears were it ever permitted the Circassian to weep for the brave.

But besides the music heard on these extraordinary occasions, the singing of ballads coupled with the telling of stories is the common entertainment of the Circassian winter evening. Then when the large logs of oak blaze on the hearth of the apartment reserved in every house for the reception of guests, and the door of which remains hospitably open throughout the day, a little company is assembled at nightfall to while away with song an hour or two before retiring to rest. The professional minstrel, who is capable of extemporizing both words and melodies, may not be present, but there will be some one, perhaps an aged blind man, or a lad skilled in music beyond his fellows, who can touch the lyre. Any person, however, happening to be present, *furore dulci plenes,* is at liberty to volunteer a song.

It may be a humorous one, pointed with quaint wit, barbed with sarcasm, seasoned with homely proverbs, and acted out with singular powers of mimicry and even of ventriloquism. But more frequently it will treat of the adventures of the hunter or the traveller, and the still graver themes of war and love. If a solo, it will often be a rapid recitative, varied at short intervals by a few tenor and bass notes thrown in by three or four other voices, and producing an effect like the swell and fall of the organ. If a trio or quartette, there will still be added from time to time a heavy bass accompaniment, a sort of fugue, and in war-songs often resembling the moaning of the sea in a storm, or the wailing over the dead brought home from the battle field. Other ballads again will be more gay and lively, with responses executed by three different parties alternately. Let whatever be the theme and whoever the performers, as the song proceeds, and the feelings of all become wrought up to the highest pitch of enthusiasm by the recital of the great deeds done in battle, or gallant sacrifices dared in love, the voices of one or more of the listeners will be sure to break into the strain; the whole audience will join in the cheerful chirrup of hai-hai-cha! or the dirge-like wail of wai-wai-wai! and at the finale some delikan, inspired perhaps by the sight of maiden faces cautiously peering in at door or window, will scarcely be able to refrain from firing his pistol up the chimney, or even through the ceiling.

How untrue the representation that a people in whose hearts lives the love of songs like these are a race of freebooters! Listening constantly to the praise of heroes, whether famous in the legends of antiquity or still living surrounded with the respect of their fellows, the soul of the young warrior is early inspired with a love for war and glory. He, too, will be a hero. He will be the first in his district, the chief of his tribe, the praise of the mountains, and the terror of the plains. He therefore goes forth to distinguish himself in the fight, and bring home trophies of his prowess. If theft is held in esteem by the Circassian, as formerly by the Spartan warrior, it is so mainly for its adroitness, a quality so necessary in circumventing the enemy; and if he exults in stripping the discomfited Muscovite and Cossack of their arms and clothing, these are the tokens of his valor, and chiefly as such are prized by him.

XIV.

DANCES.

SCHAMYL, though from boyhood exhibiting in manners and character a certain degree of thoughtful gravity beyond his years, was, like all his countrymen, a dancer. Nor does the Circassian dance require, for the most part, any levity of disposition in the performer; some varieties of it being practised as a martial exercise, and with a decorum bordering on seriousness. In the war-dance the Lesghian, more particularly, is imperious in look as well as animated in action. He carries himself haughtily through all the evolutions, moving with equal grace and rapidity, keeping perfect time in his complicated steps, exhibiting an elasticity of tread, a suppleness of limbs, and a vigor of body truly astonishing; while at the same time the fierce earnestness of his countenance and his noble bearing are, as it were, a challenge to his enemies. Among European dances this warlike figure most resembles the highland fling of Scotland.

The dancing of the women appears tame and monotonous in comparison. Theirs is a slow movement, the principal charm of which is in its grace, and which requires for its execution a certain undulating motion of the body rather than any extra exertion of the feet and legs.

At all public festivals the two sexes always dance together. Generally after supping on roasted sheep or sodden kid, together with cakes of pastry and the aromatic honey, followed on the part of the male portion of the company by brimming bowls of mead, they form a ring on the greensward for their favorite pastime and crowning pleasure of the feast. The circle is often a very large one, with a bonfire in the centre during the evening. The daughters unveiled, are led down from their tents, situated a little apart on the hill-side, by their carefully muffled mothers, who with a prudence characteristic of them in other lands, also generally select from the candidates for the estate of matrimony such partners as may best suit both the present proprieties and the future possibilities of the case. Without a trifle of coquetry there is no dancing even in Circassia. The pipers then having taken their places, strike up a merry measure, to which moves gracefully round the whole circle. The beaux are expected to look grave as judges or the council ring itself, but the movement allows of a good deal of jamming and squeezing; so much so, indeed, that the fair ones are not unfrequently taken off their feet and borne around for short distances by the force of the pressure. When they touch the ground, however, their robes being short and their trowsers tightly fastened above the ancle, the movement of their feet, which are almost always pretty, is shown off to advantage.

It is a truly pleasing sight, the dance on the green of the valley, by daytime beneath the wide spread shade of aged oaks, in the twilight by the light of the harvest moon at its full, or with only the stars of night aided by the blazing pile of logs to illumine the scenes; while the long frocks of the deli-kans wave in concert with the skirts of the maidens, and youthful pleasure trips on tiptoe around the ring.

There is also the clown's dance, generally executed at entertainments after the mead or *boza* has worked sufficiently on the brain to produce a moderate degree of hilarity. It commences with a measured clapping of hands; a few low notes succeed, which, as the audience joins in, swell into a lively air; when some wild-looking "ghilly" in a long, tattered coat springs into the centre of the circle and begins shuffling. As he proceeds the singing grows gradually louder, accompanied from time to time with a more violent clapping of hands. Even shouts and screams are occasionally added to spur him on. Excited to the highest pitch of enthusiasm he then hops about with vigor, springing on the very points of his toes, and spinning around with great velocity, until suddenly down he drops flat on the green with strange ventriloquial sounds, mingled with moans as if the fall had half killed him. Then he throws off a volley of witty impromptus which set the ring in a roar of laughter; to these are added comical imitations of the cries of various animals; next he addresses some chieftain present in a strain of mock eloquence; and finally, the laughing devil leaping out of his eye, ends his buffoonery with dealing a pretty good whack or two over the shoulders of the most reverend seignor in the company, who, if he himself is a serf, may be his own master.

Frequently the dancer accompanies his motions more or less with his voice, being assisted also by the audience, who beat the measure with their hands, and chant the chorus of A-ri-ra-ri-ra. And as from time to time holding up his long garment behind with both hands, and bending his body low, he watches exultingly the movement of his feet, he shouts aloud with plaintive voice as if undergoing severe pain instead of experiencing an ecstasy of delight.

When the song of the dancer runs on love and vaunts the praises of some maiden renowned for beauty, the young warriors present pledge their own sweethearts in bowls of boza, and every few minutes discharge their pistols or rifles in the air. This latter act is always regarded as a challenge to the whole company, and whoever has a charge of gunpowder left immediately burns it in honor of the superior charms of his lady-love.

The intervals of repose between the dances and songs are very naturally filled up by story-telling. For the Circassians are scarcely less fond of tales and fables than of music and the fling. Having no books they hang eagerly upon the lips of whoever is skilled in recounting story, legend, and adventure, with the gift perhaps of throwing in scraps of song, proverbs, and jests, together with occasional displays of mimicry, feats in ventriloquism, grimaces, whistling, chirruping, and ringing all the changes of laughter. The winter evening's log burns to embers while some clever, sweet-tongued narrator repeats some of the thousand and one tales of the war against the Russians, or recites the adventures of the chase on the Terek and in the higher Caucasus, or dwells in turn now upon the ancient traditions of the tribes, and now on the wonders which the recent traveller has beheld in Tiflis, Constantinople, or St. Petersburg.

The imagination of the mountaineer is ardent, however simple may be his own manner of life, and he loves especially to hear of the marvels of either eastern or western magnificence; so that when after an evening spent in listening to such recitals he lays his head upon his mat or his saddle, it is full to bursting of hanging gardens and marble palaces, high towers and the minarets of mosques, the gorgeous ceremonies of courts, the array and glitter of parades, and the gaudy street-pageants and bustle of affairs in the great metropolitan capitals of the plains.

XV.

FESTIVALS.

THE Circassian year was pretty well crowded with festivals until recently, when the introduction of the Mahometan doctrines put an end to a good many of the merry usages of paganism. The hearts of the people continuing to cling with tenacity, however, to what was most pleasing in the ancient superstitions, there are still left a considerable number of the old festal ceremonies and observances. At new year, at the beginning and ending of the March moon, at the gathering of the harvest, as well as on many minor occasions throughout the year, the people assemble to hold their sacred feasts, when for lack of priests the aged and most revered warriors present to the divinities the prayers of the congregation; the goat, the sheep, or the ox is sacrificed, and afterward feasted upon; libations of mead are poured, though less upon the ground than down the throats of the worshippers; while unleavened bread and cheese-cakes are devoured with a voraciousness very little akin to devotion. Dances, songs, and stories are duly intermingled; also racing, wrestling, and leaping; and finally, the solemnity is closed with exercises in sharp-shooting, and the discharge of firearms in the air.

The season immediately following the harvest when the wheat, the millet, and the corn have been garnered up in the storehouses, and the winter's fodder for the cattle has been stacked in the fields, is especially a time of merry-making. An unusual joy also attends the labors of securing the crops. For the mowers sing their national airs in the meadows, and keep time with the sweep of their scythes. Sometimes at the commencement of the hay-harvest they may be seen going into the fields in parties of fifties; and any company of travellers happening then to be passing by will be good-naturedly attacked with both scythes and shouts, pulled from their horses, and carried off in triumph. For their ransom they will have to give at least a sheep to help out the evening's supper, besides honey enough to make mead for the whole company. And with such a prospect of feasting before them the laborers will return with increased zest to their work, swinging gaily their short scythes worn well-nigh to the backbone, roaming in parties hither and thither through the field, and attacking, amid songs and shoutings, the thickest masses of grass as if so many Russian *corps d'armée.*

A pleasing rural sight indeed it is, the green valley glowing in the warm sunlight, and its grass coarse, but savory to the cattle, lying in heavy swaths, or piled in stacks. Mixed with this are the juicy chicory-stalks eight or ten feet in height, and tipped with light blue flowers. The sweet clover also, of both the white and red varieties, is scattered more or less among the taller grasses; so that the meadow is as fragrant as a bank of wild flowers, or a parterre in a garden.

With rejoicings somewhat similar is the return of seed-time celebrated, except it is then the time for hopes instead of thanksgivings. And the joy felt at this season when, the time of the singing of birds having come and the voice of the turtle being heard in the land, the grain is committed in faith of increase to the earth, is the greater in consequence of a period of partial abstinence and renunciation of social pleasures, analogous to the Christian lent, having preceded it. For during the month of March the Circassian puts himself on a low diet, refraining especially from the eating of eggs, and will neither hire, lend, borrow, or receive any thing from another, not even a light from a neighbor's house. So general seems to be the prompting of nature in favor of a period of fasting at the commencement of the spring. But the March moon once set there is immediately held a feast, at which what few of the eggs laid by in the course of the month preceding have not already in the course of the day been devoured, are fired at as a mark, and when the skins of the victims slain at the festival become the reward of the conquerors.

There is no great variety in the Circassian festivals, for whatever be the object of them, there is the same roasting of sheep and oxen, the same singing and dancing, the same mark-firing, horse-racing, and athletic games. The private feasts, also, are accompanied with amusements very similar in character, excepting that there is generally a very long succession of dishes, with interchange of presents between hosts and guests, and also with the difference that religious ceremonies are practised only on the more public occasions, the Circassian having, at least before the introduction of Mahometanism, no domestic worship, nor guiding his personal conduct by any religious sentiments separate from his sense of duty in the domestic and social relations, his feeling of honor, and love of country.

XVI.

HIS RELIGIOUS EDUCATION.

THE principal part of the early training of Schamyl consisted in daily practising the games and warlike exercises of his countrymen; but there was besides the important teaching received from Dschelal Eddin. The latter had begun when the boy was still of tender age giving him lessons in the Arabic tongue and grammar; and through a period of several years had continued expounding to him, probably in a class with others, the wisdom of the Koran, until he was sufficiently advanced in its knowledge to be appointed to chant it in the messdshed during divine service. Still later he instructed his intelligent pupil in the Mahometan literature and philosophy; no doubt, with acute elucidation of definitions and first principles, with learned comments on the maxims of the Sunnite and Sufite doctors, and with various illustrations of the character of the principal writers in oriental science and fiction, both Arabic and Persian. For the Daghestan teachers of theology, called ulemas or murschids, are not without repute for both subtilty and erudition; and Dschelal Eddin was one of the most learned among them.

Like most of these professors the sage of Himri was one of the sect of the Sufis; and it was their view of the Mahometan system of doctrine which he made it the burden of his lectures to explain and impress upon the mind of his pupil.

At first, the latter was indoctrinated in the law of externals which is called the Scharyat, and is to be observed alike by all Moslems. It prescribes prayers, almsgivings, fasting, pilgrimages, and ablutions, besides various rules to be observed in all the domestic and social relations. This is the common law of Mahometanism, the requirements of which are supposed to be universally known, and may be complied with, at least in the letter, without either learning or piety.

Next was explained to him the higher law of the Tarykat, or "path" to perfection. The knowledge of this is not for the common people, but for those only who endeavor to obey the commands of Allah, not as external ordinances and ceremonies, but because they appreciate their justness, and who practise virtue not merely for the promise of reward, but also from a sincere admiration of its nature, and delight in its exercise. These alone are worthy of being initiated into the mystery of the tarykat.

But the path to truth is not the truth itself. As only he who perseveres and pushes onward in a race finally arrives at the goal, so only by the continued and disinterested pursuit of truth is it finally found, and the Sufi attains to the third stage in the spiritual life which is called the Hakyat. To reach this exalted condition of humanity the disciple must restrain all his natural passions and moderate all his desires. In the denial of self he must labor for the good of others. Whatever contributes to refine the feelings, to exalt the thoughts, to extend the knowledge of the spiritual world, is to be desired; while the lust of the flesh, the lust of the eye, and the pride of life are to be as earnestly repressed and mortified. The seeker after the truth finds it only by frequent meditation amid the solitude of nature. Thither he will go both to study the pages of the sacred books and to decipher the scroll of his own inner consciousness. Thither also will he repair to commune with the one universal spirit which pervades all things, but which reveals itself especially to those who seek for it in the deep stillness of the forests, among the rocks of the mountains, and by the secluded waterfalls and fountains. In this high communion alone is it that man arrives at the perfection of which his nature is capable.

The state of the hakyat fully attained, man has to take but one step more and he is perfect even as God is perfect. This is the state called the Maarifat. For whoever has passed through the preceding degrees of perfection will at last be favored with intuitions in which, being in ecstasy, his spirit will mingle with the infinite spirit, and humanity will become divinity. To this condition of ecstasy the Sufis give the name of *h'al.* In it meditation having been carried so far as to result in apathy and a total loss of self-consciousness, the flesh having been to such a degree mortified and annihilated as to admit of a temporary separation of the spirit from the body, and the personal self being so completely relieved of the limitations of time and space that it returns to its normal condition of universality, then the soul of the Sufi and the soul of Allah are one. Both are infinite, all-knowing, impersonal, and the only reality. Whoever has thus beheld the unveiled face of God is ever after superior to the law of externals, and is guided entirely by the inner light of reason. He fears no punishment and is influenced by no hope of reward, save the sting and approval of his own conscience. When he gives alms it is not because the scharyat prescribes, but his own heart prompts it; if he practises washings it is also not because he is required so to do by the Koran, but from himself regarding cleanliness as next to godliness. Henceforth his soul is vexed by no doubts respecting spiritual truth; he is exposed to no errors of faith; he is elevated to a state of beatitude which is even independent of the performance of good works; and being made a partaker of the unity of the divine nature he knows no further distinction of sects, but regards the true believers of all creeds as brethren. "Whoso," say the Habistan, "does not acknowledge that it is indifferent whether he is a Mussulman or a Christian, has not raised himself to the truth, and knows not the essence of being."

Such in brief was the system of religious doctrine which Schamyl learned sitting at the feet of Dschelal Eddin. But that it was fully adopted by him in the heyday of youth and in possession of an intellect as penetrating as his feeling was ardent, is not to be believed. More or less of its influence, however, may be seen in the habits of temperance and frugality uniformly maintained by him, in his perfect self-control, in his love for contemplation amid the solitude of nature, as well as by his subsequently making it, at least theoretically, the rule of his life and the basis of his system of policy.

XVII.

HIS MARRIAGE.

THE age at which Schamyl took a wife is not known; but probably it was not over that of twenty-one. Nor, although later in life his harem consisted of three ladies, one of whom was a beautiful young Armenian, can any positive information be given respecting the character or person of the one espoused first. In accordance with Circassian usages she might have been selected by his atalik from the class of maidens in Himri whose circumstances in life were not unlike his own; or which is perhaps more likely to have been the case, she might have been one who was preferred by the young man himself from his having been smitten by her grace in the dance on the green, or having received from her fair hands the embroidered scarf won as a prize in the games.

However this might have been, the first step towards the marriage must have consisted in carrying off the girl, nothing loth doubtless, through the agency of a party of his friends. This feat successfully accomplished, though frequently it is no more than a formality and mere fiction in usage, the next thing to be done was to settle with her father or friends the price of her. The market value of a maid in Circassia depends upon both her rank and her charms. If a belle of the blood of the chieftains of a tribe in the western Caucasus, she may be worth as much as two hundred and fifty pieces of merchandise, valued at one dollar each, besides eight or ten horses and four or five serf-girls, which is more than the price formerly paid by Homer's heroes, as in the case of the

> Daughter of Ops, the just Pisenor's son,
> For twenty beeves by great Laertes won.

But it is not probable that Schamyl gave for

his wife more than a gun or a sabre, a horse or a couple of beeves. But this much it must certainly have cost him to get respectably married; for without gifts to her parents no Circassian young woman is ever given in marriage, unless in some such exceptional circumstances as when Agamemnon wishing to appease the wrath of Achilles after the robbery of Briseis proposed to replace her by one of his own daughters, and said that "far from exacting from him the accustomed presents he would endow the girl with immense riches."

This rule, however, does not apply to widows, who being considered as the property of the fraternity to which belonged the deceased husband, are given away gratis to whoever will accept of them. And while a female of this class would not fetch so much as a cow or a buffalo in the market, no man of course would ever deem it worth his while to be at the pains of the elopement.

But in the case of a maid being carried off, unless a satisfactory dowry were promptly given, a feud would arise between the parties which could scarcely be settled without bloodshed. If, however, a young man being deeply smitten with love, or for any other reason, elopes with a fair one before he has accumulated a sufficient fortune to defray the expense of such a luxury, it is common enough for him to pay down what money or valuables he may have, and give security for the remainder. The transaction being like any other in business is done in plain words, and without any pretence on the part of the suitor of being actuated solely by disinterested affection.

Once the bargain struck there is a feast. When the parties have a sufficiency of means, the relatives and friends assemble to the number perhaps of several hundreds to celebrate the betrothals by a picnic and a dance from morning till night. A master of ceremonies with a long flat baton as a symbol of authority makes his proclamation calling upon all present to lay aside their feuds, if any they have, and take their places in the dance. The musicians with three-fingered pipes and two-stringed violins are drawn up in the centre of the ring, when each gallant placing his arms under those of the damsels on either side, and interlacing his fingers with theirs, they all move slowly around in the immense circle, singing at the same time a sort of accompaniment to the instrumental music, swinging the body gracefully backwards and forwards, and rising on the toes in such a way as to communicate an undulating motion to the whole ring as it goes round. Pistols would be fired every few minutes over the heads of the dancers, and mock onsets made upon the circle by mounted horsemen, who would be driven back in turn by parties armed with branches of trees and making the air ring with their shouts. There would also be the usual horse-racing, wrestling, and running, besides the entertainment of the feast itself, which would be served by waiters on horseback as well as on foot, and who together would keep up a brisk circulation of tables and trenchers.

When finally the marriage day arrives, all dues under the matrimonial compact having been paid or satisfactorily secured, the couple are joined together with still more feasting and the observance of additional ceremonies. A friend of the bridegroom mounting on horseback and taking on his crupper the maiden decked out in all her finery, and covered with a long white veil, gallops off with her to the house of some relative where the wedding is to be celebrated. Received at the door by the matron of the house, she is conducted with grave formality to the chamber set apart for her reception, where she awaits the arrival of her lord, and lights the nuptial torch of pine sticks in order to keep away any supernatural enemy who might be tempted to run off with her at this very nick of time.

An elderly dame also now performs the mystic ceremony of walking three times around the bridal couch, repeating the while the words of some Arabic charm, and afterwards placing by the bedside three earthen-ware pots filled with corn, and containing each a a lighted lamp.

At last the hour of midnight arrived, the impatient bridegroom springing into his saddle gallops to the house of his friend, and conducted into the presence of his bride instantly rips open her corset with his poniard. This is the conclusion of the ceremony by which is rather cut than tied the Circassian knot of matrimony, there being neither priest nor magistrate employed to fasten it any more securely.

XVIII.

MAIDS.

The bride of Schamyl must have been unlike her countrywomen generally, if she was not handsome. For the Circassian females have long been famed for their beauty, not only being in demand for the supply of the Turkish harems, but having formerly been sought in marriage by the Hungarian kings and the czars of Muscovy, as well as by the Byzantine princes and the pashas of Stamboul. They are described by travellers as of good height, having slight and pliant forms like the birch among trees, with complexion either fair or olive, the old Greek cast of features, and eyes and hair generally dark, though some writers in describing them sing also of

> The eyes' blue dalliance,
> And the golden hair.

On their heads the girls wear a bonnet not unlike the Albanian skullcap, of scarlet or some other brilliant color, and trimmed with lace of silver. Beneath this their hair falls down their shoulders in braids which are confined at the end by a silver cord, or are tied like the tresses of the Cossack girls with bright ribbons that nearly sweep the ground. Sometimes also these plaits are gracefully confined in a silken network.

Over the shift is worn a jacket of some gay color and confined in front by silver clasps; or it may be simply a leathern corselet joined together by stitches. In either case the waist is incased as it were in a straight jacket, which being put on at the age of ten or even younger, and worn constantly until the marriage night, restrains the fulness of nature throughout the period of maidenhood. A skirt open in front and confined around the waist by a scarf or girdle, falls sufficiently short of the ankles to show the wide Turkish trowsers which are tied above them.

Closely fitting morocco slippers cover the feet, which being kept as scrupulously clean as those of the Hindoo women, if not like theirs ornamented with rings, are indoors frequently left bare; while out of the house a kind of wooden clogs are worn to avoid the dirt. The slippers are sufficiently coquettish, being made of red or green morocco, and of a size to admit the foot only in part, with small high heels, and dainty, pointed toes slightly turned up.

The hands, which as well as the feet are small, have the finger nails dyed with the juice of the flowers of the balsamina, and are protected in the open air by mittens. The natural colors of the face, however, are generally not heightened by the pencil, although the Circassian fair are partial to the brightest tints in their apparel, being thereto invited by the gorgeous lights of a landscape filled with a multitude of flowers and in which the very rocks and snows burn morning and evening with hues scarcely less brilliant and variegated.

The daughters of families a little elevated above the general social level, go to school in the mosques together with the boys, and are taught like them to speak and write the Turkish. At home all are instructed in the feminine arts of spinning and weaving, as well as in embroidery, the knitting of lace, the making of all articles of dress, and also the plaiting of straw mats and baskets. They often serve the guests of the master of the house, bringing water to wash the feet of the newly arrived, though not like the Mary of the Scriptures anointing them with frankincense and wiping them with the hair of the head. The aged men being like the stranger universally honored in Circassia, receive from the young maidens the most dutiful attentions; and it is always their privilege to sit by the couch of the veterans brought home wounded from the wars. The one are petted throughout their second childhood with frequent presents of sweetmeats and baskets of nuts; and the other feel their pains abated while the hands of the most beautiful of the tribe softly comb the tuft of hair left growing above their brows. But in return, these too are treated by the other sex with corresponding courtesy; for every warrior is a gallant knight, ever ready, going and returning from the foray, to give his escort to the damsel wishing to pass from hamlet to hamlet, and gracefully lifting her upon his crupper whenever by chance he meets her on foot in the valleys.

The Circassian maid is said to have in her veins some of the blood of the Amazons who anciently bore the pharetra, and followed hunting in these mountains. Her style of dress and measured gait, together with her sharing the martial sentiments of the society in which she lives, give her still something of the port of Diana, and make her fit to be the warrior's bride. But at the same time she is not lacking in the feminine graces. Dressed in brocade or in rags, the Circassian girl is represented by travellers as never awkward, and never failing to assume spontaneously the most easy and natural as well as the most dignified attitudes. Her manners have but little of the excessive reserve afterwards adopted when she becomes a wife. But so long as she is in the market for a husband, she allows herself to be seen freely by all men whether wishing or not to become purchasers. She goes abroad unveiled; dances with the other sex; mingles fearlessly though without effrontery amid the groups of men; kisses the hand of the stranger before seating herself on the divan by his side; and, though truly modest and decorous in her deportment, she yields her cheek, almost without a blush, to the lips of the warrior who, returning from the slaughter of the enemy, feels entitled to claim those favors which in less fortunate lands can only be stolen by swains the most dexterous and whose stars aid them.

The Circassian girls are sparingly nourished, says an ancient writer,* living mostly on milk, bread of millet, and pastry. Delicate in her food as she is neat in her dress, growing up in the healthy air of the mountains, living in a society of simple tastes and natural habits, always treated with gallant courtesy by a race of men whose hearts are mostly moved by a love of war and of beauty, it is not strange that nature should have preserved through so many generations something of the

* Pallas.

type of loveliness which adorned the world's age of gold, and which in modern times has made the Caucasian head to be regarded by civilized man as the truest image of his Maker.

XIX.

WIVES.

WHILE the Circassian damsel, in her modest simplicity, is tolerant of freedoms not altogether consistent with occidental notions of propriety, and is generally ready enough to flee her tribe with a lover who happens to be unable to pay the dowry demanded by a too avaricious father or guardian, on becoming a married woman she takes the veil and retires from the gaze of men almost as effectually as she would do by shutting herself up in a convent. Now when she goes abroad, all her gay colors are covered by the white mantle which envelops her whole figure. Her sanctum, if she lives in a hamlet, is separate from the other buildings, is inclosed by a wooden fence, and concealed by the foliage of trees and shrubbery. No males enter it, excepting those of her own family and the ataliks of her children. Even her husband does not visit her in the daytime, but steals to her couch under cover of the darkness of night like a paramour. When out of the house she scrupulously avoids meeting his eye, and on perceiving him in the same path goes about or stands aside in order to avoid his notice.

Having been bought with a price, she is rather the slave than the companion of her husband, who may have as many wives as he likes, or rather can pay for. She rises on his entrance into her apartments and remains standing until he is seated; and this in fact is a mark of respect paid by woman to all males, except they be serfs, but also to the elders of their own sex. Latterly, however, the introduction of Mahometanism has brought even into these mountains a partial recognition of those rights which in some western countries have recently secured for the wife the blessings of financial as well as social independence. Under the law of the

Koran she is nominally free; can hold property in her own right; and on the infringement of her privileges, may have the satisfaction of prosecuting her husband at law and bringing him into court to answer her.

The Circassian woman, however, not having as yet become accustomed to place much reliance on her legal rights, contents herself with the exercise of those means of influence, if not of control, which have been given her by nature. Denied the pleasure of the society of her lord during the day, when at evening he comes to her apartments, fatigued it may be by the exercise of the chase or the exertions of the foray, she smoothes the brows wrinkled by care, dissipates by gentle caresses the pains of overwearied nature, and wins over to the emotions of conjugal love, the soul which all day long has been vexed by angry passions and the rage of war.

As a wife she is faithful; for indeed the jealousy of a Circassian husband is not to be endured. The disgrace of being sent home to her parents and of compelling them to pay back her purchase-money, would pierce her heart like a knife; not to mention other more barbarous punishments with which the haughty warrior instantly avenges any encroachment on his honor.

She is not only dutiful, but diligent in his service. She prepares with her own hands his food; she makes all his clothes, covering them with stitches until they become a raiment of needle-work; and helped by her daughters she even manufactures his shoes and caps, his tent and shaggy cloak, besides embroidering the coverings of his arms and the trappings of his war-horse. To the Circassian woman therefore might be addressed the commands of Telemachus to Penelope:—

> Your widowed hours apart, with female toil
> And various labors of the loom, beguile.

Nor in her poverty does she refuse the severer labors of the garden and the field. Frequently she delves in the earth by the side of her Adam. Sometimes she earns in the sweat of her brows the bread of both, while he combats the invaders of their common country in pass and plain, or practises his athletic games in the peaceful valley, or even sits idle by the house-door, interrupting his listlessness only to burnish a weapon or caress his steed. And in the higher and more barren mountains, if the reports of travellers are to be credited, his better half, as modest and still more industrious than the first mother, may be seen picking the flinty soil during the heats of the day decked out with none of the finery worn on occasions of ceremony, but clad simply in that one garment deemed indispensable in all countries having made the smallest progress in civilization.*

The headdress of the married woman is not the tiara of the maid, but some kind of plain or ornamental stuff wound round the head in the form of a turban, and with ends falling gracefully down on the shoulders. This completely covers the hair which is worn short, with curls in the neck. Over it on going out is thrown a veil of snow-white muslin which descending mingles its folds with those of the mantle. This latter is often a large square of European woollen of the finest texture that can be afforded by the wearer; and whether fine or coarse has always a picturesque look in the distance; and nearer by

* Dubois.

is generally worn with a certain degree of womanly coquetry which lends grace to its folds, and to the dullest eyes reveals half-glimpses of the beauty concealed beneath.

Here the fashions of dress, whether for males or females, never change. Garments therefore not being thrown aside or altered with every month's variation of style as in the west, are frequently made of costly materials and adorned with such elegance of needle-work as to render them almost as precious as the sacred poet's vesture of gold wrought about with divers colors. This applies of course to garments of ceremony chiefly. A very fine paraja or mantle of camel or goat's hair, a skirt of brocade, or a scarf ornamented with silver thread will sometimes outlast a generation, and be handed down an heirloom even to grandchildren. The belle who putting on the apparel which possibly a preceding century has fabricated, does not find herself in an antiquated cut nor with stitches placed amiss, loses no time of course in dreaming of new fashions, nor self-respect in being obliged to parade in the old ones. Her only fashionable foible is that of knitting silver lace, she not having as yet been initiated into the mystery of making Chinese boxes and card-racks, dolls' dresses and family portraits in worsted.

XX.

FEMALE SLAVE-TRADE.

Serfdom, to a limited extent, exists in the Caucasus, more particularly in the western part. It is, however, a comparatively mild form of bondage, the only real slaves in the mountains being the captives taken in war who are compelled to do most of the hewing of wood and the drawing of water. The serfs are rarely transferred with the land, and never without their own consent. In return for their services they receive maintenance, clothing, lodging, and some yearly gratuity. Wives are furnished them gratis; and while their sons remain the serfs of the master, the money received for the daughters when sold in marriage is equally divided between him and the father. Their occupations consist in cultivating the soil, taking care of horses and cattle, and waiting in the guest-house; they being under no obligation to serve in war or even give attendance on journeys. Often they farm the land of their masters for half the product. They also have the right of purchasing their freedom at the price of a certain number of oxen; and if ill-treated may flee to another master for protection, who on payment of a moderate compensation to their former owner is entitled to retain them. Socially they are on a footing of almost equality with their lords, wearing the same dress, living in similar houses, partaking of about the same diet, sharing in all games and festivities, and associating on all occasions with freemen as if they were their peers.

The well-known Circassian slave-trade is confined to the sale of females. In the eastern Caucasus girls are rarely bought and sold except in marriage; but in the western they are exported to supply the harems of the Turks, more especially those of Constantinople. At one time this trade was forbidden by

Russia, and all of her subjects found engaged in it were sent to Siberia; but in 1845 it was again legalized on condition that the females to be exported into Turkey should take out letters of Russian protection, the object being partly to conciliate the Circassians, and partly to create a class of persons resident in the dominions of the sultan who should depend upon the czar as their protector and lord paramount.

Even when prohibited, however, the traffic was carried on by means of small craft which under protection of Russian papers obtained at Trebizond under pretence of going to Kertsch for grain, braved the dangers of the winter voyage when from the inclemency of the weather the Russian cruisers had been withdrawn from the coast of Circassia, and taking in their precious cargo of souls landed it at Sinope or Samsoun. Thence conducted privately to Trebizond, they were finally conveyed by Turkish and Austrian steamers to Constantinople.

These girls were the daughters of the serfs and poorer class of persons; those of nobles, chiefs, and men of means being rarely if ever sold to the slave-merchant. Sold they however must be even if they remain at home, the Asiatic doctrine prevailing in the Caucasus that the woman should be bought, not given in marriage, and where a dowry in addition to a wife would be the gilding of refined gold and adding sugar to the honey-comb. The married woman is the property of her lord — or was until nominally set free by the introduction of the law of the Koran. The idea of becoming the slave of a master was therefore nearly synonymous in the mind of a maid of low degree with that of becoming the wife of a husband; and to make the journey to Constantinople for the purpose of being bought by a wealthy Turk, was looked forward to by many a one as a settlement in life preferable to remaining at home the wife of a poor peasant. This sentiment was encouraged by the sight, not uncommon in Circassia, of females who after having obtained an education and a competency in Constantinople have returned to reside in their own country. It is also well known to the humblest maiden that the high officers in the Turkish state often take to themselves wives of the daughters of the Caucasus, who, if they do not return to the land of their fathers, at least play, in that of their adoption, a part in society superior to that of the wives of even chiefs and princes in the mountains.

Accordingly, it is not generally looked upon by the Caucasian female born in poverty, as a misfortune to be sold into Turkish captivity. She pleases her fancy, on the contrary, with imagining that she will become the wife of, it may be, the sultan himself, or of a pasha, or of the admiral of the fleet. She will be the light of the harem of a nabob with many tails. She will be dressed in rich silks and velvets, and adorned with gold and jewelry. She will live in the great aoul of Stamboul, in a sakli by the Golden Horn, or in the woods that skirt the Sweet Waters. Nor, poor thing, does she know or stop to consider that she may be thrown into those same beautiful waters sewed up alive in a sack. Many a one, no doubt, leaves her home however humble with a sigh of regret; many a one sheds bitter tears of shame when made to stand forth half naked in the market-place; and many a one even in the gorgeous halls and perfumed chambers of Constantinopolitan princes, tired of the watching of eunuchs and of the bickerings of rivals, would gladly exchange all the luxuries of the harem for the freedom of a hut in her native mountains.

Still it is the testimony of travellers that the great majority of poor females in Circassia are as ready to go to Stamboul as pilgrims to Mecca. When captured by Russian cruisers on the voyage, some of them have been known to cast themselves into the sea or to drive a knife into their hearts rather than submit to become wives to the enemies of their country, the hated Muscovites; but they have no aversion to the Turk. Often they suffer somewhat on the voyage for lack of suitable shelter, food, and clothing; and generally they arrive at Constantinople much better subjects for the Turkish bath than the harem. But they are often placed in seminaries to be educated for the places they are to occupy in the houses of the great; being on their arrival frequently not more than twelve years of age, and always destitute of the few accomplishments considered indispensable in the families of Turks of any distinction. A beautiful young Circassian, when thus prepared for the life of the harem, will sometimes sell for as much as twenty or even thirty or forty thousand piastres, though the ordinary price might not be more than five or ten thousand. But even in Circassia an Englishman has been known to pay for a wife "three hundred and twenty-five pieces of cotton cloth," valued there at upwards of six thousand piastres. Since the repeal of the Russian law forbidding the slave-trade, however, the price of this merchandise has greatly fallen in the market.

There is no evil, however great, without some good; and to the Circassian trade in female slaves is to be traced the superiority, both of physiognomy and of blood, which belongs to the modern Turk above the Tartar of the steppe and of the desert.

XXI.

FORM OF GOVERNMENT.

The society of which Schamyl on reaching the age of manhood became a member in full was a free democracy. In the western Caucasus the various tribes, such as the Kabardians, the Ubighé, and the Adighé, who are the Circassians proper, live under a form of social organization more or less feudal and aristocratic; but in the eastern, among the Lesghians, the Tchetchenians, and the inhabitants of Daghestan, there is for the most part no distinction of classes. Several small tribes in this latter division which are of Tartar origin are indeed governed by khans; but even among them where the form of government is despotic, as well as west of the Terek where it is aristocratic, there prevails such a spirit of personal independence together with such an equality of civil rights and social conditions, that the Circassians in general may best be characterized as associations of free brothers, not unlike the Germans as described by Tacitus.

More especially is this true of the Lesghians of whom is Schamyl. Among them previously to the establishment of his system of government, there was no other chief of the state than he who by general consent led the warriors of the tribe on their expeditions against the enemy. Nor did such office of leader outlast a foray or a campaign. In time of peace all were brothers, free and equal before the law, with only such diversity of social condition as might result from a difference in natural gifts or in the favors of fortune. Whoever had been endowed with most commanding powers, whoever was foremost in valor and the exercise of all manly virtues, was in fact a chieftain though without the formality of an election; he was king though without a title; and between the natural and the divine right to govern there was practically no difference.

The public affairs of the tribe were regulated in general assembly. The freemen came together at their own will to sit in the council ring on the greensward beneath the trees. In these meetings no officer claimed precedence as a right, but all granted it by consent to the elders and those most distinguished for valor and the gift of speech. The counsels of age and experience were heard first. The wise man also, whoever he was, the valiant in arms, the influential from worth of character, all gave their opinion; but most the assembly hung upon the sweet tongue of eloquence. For the orator has ample scope in the free assemblies of the Circassians. When he rises to speak, especially if he be advanced in years, the principal men of the tribe sometimes even come forward and reverently kiss his robe. If possessed of more of the impetuosity of early life, he will perhaps dash into the ring on horseback and harangue the assembly from the saddle. Then if in the midst of his impassioned volubility any Hotspur interrupt the orator, the latter foams with rage and would transgress all bounds of propriety if the lifted hand of some elder did not instantly restore silence.

When the object of the meeting is to agree on an expedition against the enemy, the favorite topic and constant burden of eloquence is the oppression and the cruelty of the Russians. As the speaker dilates upon their burnings and shedding of blood, the aoul laid low by their artillery, the women violated, the youth carried away captive, the tribes gradually driven back into the mountains, his voice rages with indignation or wails in the plaintive tones of unaffected sorrow. His eye flashes beneath the shaggy, contracted brows; the clenched fist is relaxed only to grasp shaska or poniard; the blood rushes and returns from the cheek; and the chest heaves with violently struggling emotions. Meanwhile in reply is heard the low, half-stifled sob; the irrepressible tears trickle down the sunburnt cheeks of those who weep for their country, if not their friends; teeth are clenched and brows are knit and sabres are half-drawn; while at intervals is responded amen! amen! and at the conclusion a shout of applause breaks from the universal throat, and rings through the air until the echoing hill-sides give it back to each other in boisterous accord.

New laws are rarely made by this assembly, the tribe being governed very much by custom and ancient usage. Whenever these prove an insufficient rule of action, the Koran, in those parts of the mountains where it has been introduced, is appealed to. Of course, in a state of society so simple and unchanging there is little need of that constant law-making and unmaking deemed so indispensable in free and more civilized communities. Whatever rules of conduct have been longest established and found to meet the necessities of many generations, are by these primitive mountaineers held most sacred. To execute laws, therefore, not to make them, is the prinpal object of what little government exists in the Caucasus. Offenders are tried in the council ring; punishments consist mostly of fines, which if not paid by the guilty individual himself, must be by his family or his tribe; and crimes against persons which are not thus compounded are prosecuted by the injured party and those of his blood even to the third and fourth generations.

Hence arise those numerous feuds which, arraying family against family and tribe against tribe, produce a degree of mutual alienation of which great use has been made by the Russians in their war of subjugation. For the right of revenge is one of the three great principles on which is based the whole system of Circassian usage, the exercise of hospitality and respect for age being the two others. But to limit the sway of this old law of an eye for an eye and a tooth for a tooth under which intestine wars prevailed, as formerly among the clans of Scotland, and suits at law were protracted from generation to generation, as in the chancery of England, fraternities have latterly been established and oaths imposed on the members, whereby the ends of justice have been better secured as well as domestic peace greatly promoted. For an oath taken over even a few amulets is sufficient to secure the fulfilment of an engagement; and when formally administered upon the Koran suspended from two rifle-rests, the warrior, who never trembled before, is, by the simple ceremony, agitated with dread, and having deposited his rifle, his pistol, or his bow, will die but what he will keep his word.

The barbarity of this law of blood has also been always more or less counteracted by the affectionate respect for age, wherever met with, which runs through the code of Circassian manners, as well as by such an universal practice of hospitality as keeps the door of the apartment for guests standing wide open from one end of the year to the other throughout the mountains, and which enables even the foreigner to enter the country unharmed, by placing himself under the protection of any chieftain he may select for his konak or guardian.

XXII.

RELIGIOUS BELIEF.

THE religious belief of the countrymen of Schamyl formerly partook of the simplicity of their mode of government. Not a century ago they were almost entirely pagan, performing their religious ceremonies not in temples made with hands, but in groves, in the shadow of whose melancholy boughs dwelt many divinities. They believed also in one Great Spirit whose presence filled immensity, and who was likened to no living thing, nor fashion of a man. To him were subject all inferior powers who presided over the seasons of the year, over various localities, over the lives of the lower animals, and over all the doings and destinies of mankind.

Merissa, for example, was the protector of bees; and at her festivals, celebrated at the season of gathering in the sweets of the hive, all the viands and beverages with which the worshippers regaled themselves, were prepared with honey. Still more powerful was Seozeres, who held in subjection the winds and waters, and who being at the same time the guardian of animals, tempered the air to the shorn flock and brought the springs out of the rocks for the supply of the herd. Tliebse had the care of smiths and all the cunning workmanship of forges, and at his fete libations were poured in honor of him upon the hatchet and the ploughshare. Domestic happiness and good-fellowship among neighbors were presided over by the three sisters denominated fates in the mythology of the Greeks, and who besides interfered on the field of battle to throw their invisible shield over the favorite warrior; who sped the traveller on his way; and to whom the father on bringing his family across a new threshold offered sacrifice and invocation.

Most of the religious festivals were celebrated at either seed-time or harvest. In the first instance, when the grain was scattered over the furrows in the hope that the land would yield its increase, the sower supplicated the friendly interposition of the heavenly powers; in the latter, after having laid up in storehouses the winter's supply of corn and wine, the reaper returned thanks to the celestial givers of all good things, and made merry with his friends in feasts. Nor at this season, when the sight of nature's decay dashes with a certain degree of sadness even the hilarity of the ingathering of crops did the pious mountaineers forget their dead, but uniting with the autumn which spreads over the graves the gorgeous pall of its many-colored leaves, they likewise strewed there whatever wild flowers bloomed in the mountains so late in the year. For they, too, believed in the life beyond the tomb, wherein there should be no *fana Muscov* to infest the mountains of happiness, and where the warrior, laying aside his rifle and his bow, should hear no more of war beyond the home-march at beat of which he would enter within the gates of paradise.

Various attempts have been made to introduce Christianity among these tribes, though with little success. If asked at what period was made the first one, the Circassian replies with an air of indifference, *Allah billeer*,—*God knows!* There is an old tradition that the religion of Jesus was first taught here by St. Matthew, an opinion which may have had its origin in the fact that the form of cross which is called by his name is sometimes found in the mountains. Others attribute the first bringing in of the gospel to the crusaders who, having survived the disasters of their expedition to the holy land, fled hither for refuge. For some of the smaller Osetian tribes still wear on their garments the Maltese cross in red cloth, and paint the figure of the same on their iron bucklers. At any rate the Christian cross is well known at the present day, in many parts of the Caucasus, where it is found in stone erected in solitary places, but oftener of metal suspended from the branches of oak trees. In this situation it is found accompanied by numerous votive offerings, and is an object of sincere though blind adoration. In more recent times the Russians have endeavored to impose their form of religion on those tribes who have come under the yoke of their dominion; and since the middle of the sixteenth century the Tartars, in disputing with the Muscovites for the possession of the Caucasus, have likewise taken more or less pains to introduce the doctrines of the Koran. This endeavor has been followed up by the Turks also, whose missionaries have finally succeeded in converting most of the tribes to at least nominal Mahometanism. Indeed the mountaineer was always strongly inclined to accept the fatalistic dogma so generally prevalent in the East, and now sums up his faith in the saying, "Every thing is *kismet*, destiny; and a man, whatever his inclinations, must bow to fate. Such is the will of Allah."

Still, the new faith has taken stronger hold of the chiefs and magistrates than of the main body of the people, whose heart remains, in no small degree, pagan. The popular sympathies everywhere cling to the old superstitions and the time-hallowed ceremonies. Some of the small tribes on the Caspian, continue to turn with feelings akin to adoration towards the rising and the setting sun, while on the promontory of Apsheron the white-robed priests still maintain the sacred service of their fires. The people like also to keep the merry feasts kept by their fathers before them. They love their mead and the wine forbidden by the prophet. The venerable oaks beneath which they have been accustomed to worship are still looked upon with awe, and in the murmuring of the boughs of the sacred groves the popular imagination still hears the footfalls of the divinities as did Adam those of God when in the cool of the day he walked in the garden of Eden.

XXIII.

OCCUPATIONS.

The Circassians still entertain the ancient nomadic idea that the soil is common property. Occupancy, however, gives a title for the time being; and individuals consider the land enclosed or improved by them as their own. But it is usage that no person shall claim more land than he can fairly occupy; and at his decease it is either divided equally among his sons, or is enjoyed by them in common. This, nevertheless, does not prevent the chiefs and nobles in certain parts of the country from cultivating considerable tracts by means of serfs and captives, to whom in many instances are supplied the means and appliances of farming on condition of their making return of one half of the products in kind. Nor is the lot of these laborers a hard one; for oftener will they be seen racing, wrestling, pitching quoits, and sleeping under the hedges and wattled fences than bending over the short-tailed plough or hoe.

Agriculture, in its season, is prosecuted with such a degree of diligence, however, as suffices to supply the few simple wants of the mountaineer. The soil of the valleys and river bottoms, which are cleared by setting fire to the long grass and brushwood, generally yields a large increase of every species of grain. Here also cotton, tobacco, indigo, and the vine are indigenous; many of the fruits of the most favored climes of Europe are found wild in the woods, as the peach, the pear, and the cherry; almonds and nuts of various kinds abound; the olive yields its oil; the mulberry feeds the silkworm; the fig-tree is purple with fruit; the pomegranate ripens its crimson pulp; the palm does not refuse its dates; and, in short, in the vales and slopes which extend from the level of the steppes up to the snow-line of the mountains there is almost every variety of grain and fruit which grows between the tropics and the poles.

But though the soil, watered by innumerable streams and irrigated by the springs of the mountains, is exceedingly productive, the implements of husbandry are all of the rudest. The plough with its short and almost perpendicular handles, its flat and arrow-shaped share, barely scratches the ground; the coarse but sweet grasses are mown with a stubbed scythe; and the wains are heard creaking through the hills on revolving axles, with wheels hewn out of solid pieces of wood, and in every respect as primitive as those used by Priam and his Trojans. Nor less so are the sledges for transporting hay down from the upper mountains; for they consist of a long limb of a tree trimmed on one side, while upon the branches of the other is reared the conical stack which, when the snow has fallen in winter, is easily drawn down into the valleys.

Agricultural operations are performed by aid of oxen, mules, and asses, but not by the horse, this animal being held in too much esteem to be employed in any way except under the saddle. There is an exception to this, however, in the case of threshing grain, which, as in patriarchal times, is done by driving half a dozen horses at full gallop around a little circular paddock used as a threshing-floor. In grinding the corn, too, horses are employed to turn the wheel; though the lighter seeds, such as millet, are generally ground by the women in handmills similar to those mentioned in the Christian Scriptures.

The Circassians are not only tillers of the soil, but also keepers of flocks and herds. Indeed they are no less proud of the sheep and cattle on their thousand hills than were the patriarchs who anciently pitched their tents between the Tigris and the Euphrates, or in the pleasant valleys of the land of promise. Multitudes of black, long-haired goats browse among the rocks; white broad-tailed sheep nibble the plants of the hill-sides; small oxen of the Hungarian dun color graze in the valleys; the larger buffaloes wallow in the marshes; and herds of horses, tame or half wild, roam freely through woods and pastures. The more wealthy herdsmen count their animals by hundreds; and a few even by thousands.

The two principal ornamental arts and mysteries in the Caucasus are those of the armorer and the saddler. Upon the weapons of the warrior and the trappings of his steed are spared neither pains nor expense. Beautiful designs are traced on the sword-blades, which also are unsurpassed for temper; their hilts and those of poniards are mounted with jewels; the stocks of rifles and pistols are inlaid with gold, silver, brass, and mother-of-pearl; while saddles and bridles are wrought with a profusion of nicely set stitches, with precious stones, and metals, besides being set off with toys and various tinsel.

In addition to the smiths employed in the maintenance and repair of arms there are but few artificers. For every family constructs its own house and most of its furniture, which last, excepting the necessary iron pots and wooden platters for cooking and serving meals, consists simply of a few stools, benches, chests, small round tripod tables, mattresses, cushions, coverlets, and mats. In the plaiting of these last the Circassians especially excel, and while they annually receive many stuffs from Turkey and Persia, they send back in return considerable numbers of these articles woven of the flags of the Kuban and the Terek.

The principal foreign trade of the country consists of such imports as salt, gunpowder, cottons, woollens, silks, silver thread, needles, small mirrors, drugs, coffee, Turkish soap, dried figs, raisins, lead, steel, iron, both in bars and manufactured; and of such exports as skins, furs, wax, honey, chestnuts, tallow, woods, grain, and tobacco. This interchange of commodities is effected mostly by the way of the two seas; although strings of camels, piled high with merchandise, the property of Armenians, may occasionally be seen wending their way through the mountains, and going on also to gladden the daughters of the northern steppes with the gay silks, shawls, and carpets of the south.

XXIV.

MANNERS.

THE manners of the Circassians are characterized by a remarkable degree of natural politeness. In social intercourse they rarely indulge in unseemly levity, or violate their rules, though simple, of goodbreeding and manly behavior. Even their dances and games are executed with a certain degree of decorous reserve; and on their warlike expeditions their habitual sedateness, and proud sense of self-respect, stand very much in the place of military discipline.

Their mode of salutation is by raising the right hand to the head, and sometimes lifting their caps. It is also a mark of high respect to kiss the hand of a stranger of distinction and place it on the forehead. They strike hands together in token of amity; and females part from each other by a gentle embrace with their right arms, and then a clasping of their right hands. While in addressing each other the men make use of what we call the Christian name, and whatever the difference of rank, treat each other generally with the familiarity of brothers. Still, they never fail to do honor to a chief by half rising from their seat on his entrance into a room, and by standing up erect in case he be of superior age. If, however, while sitting at meat he at any time decline the proffered bowl of mead or wine, it will very likely be offered to any elderly serf who may be standing by, though clothed in rags; nor would any guest at the feast disdain to add to the gift a portion from his own dish of meat or pastry.

This respect for age, taking the place of that for rank, runs through the whole style of Circassian manners. The decision of an aged man settles all minor controversy; when he speaks in the council ring the most loquacious keep silence; if in anger he strike a blow even, it is not returned; wherever he moves the crowd make way for him; in winter his is the warmest corner by the fireside; in summer the young girls spread his mat on the verandah and fan his slumbers; it is an honor to light his chibouque; when he wishes to ride every one is ready to saddle his steed, and a dozen lads run to help him down on his return. "Doubly accursed," says the Circassian proverb, "is the man that draweth down upon himself the malediction of the aged."

In his hospitality the Caucasian vies with the Arab of the desert. A house, or at least an apartment, is kept ready by every man of substance for the reception of strangers, its door never being closed by day, and a pile of logs always blazing on the hearth in winter evenings. The guest of distinction on arriving is assisted to alight by his host, who says to him on crossing the threshold, "Henceforth consider my father as thy father and my mother as thy mother." He then with his own hands relieves the stranger of his arms and hangs them on the wall. As sung the ancient Grecian bard—

And now with friendly force his hand he grasped,
Then led him in within his palace halls;

His coat of mail and glittering helm unclasped,
And hung the splendid armor on the walls;
For there Ulysses' arms, neglected, dim,
Are left, nor more the conqueror's crown will win.

Only after repeated solicitations on the part of the guest, and when all others present have taken their seats, will the host consent to sit down himself; and even then he will crouch down at a respectful distance on the floor. After the repast, served perhaps by the sons of the house, water is brought in by maid-servants, that the guest may wash his hands while they carefully do the same office for his feet. In a corner of the room, or by the side of the hearth in winter, is spread a silken couch, with a luxurious pile of cushions and coverlets brought from Turkey or Persia; while sometimes a member of the family sleeps on guard by the door way.

Departing, the distinguished guest is accompanied out of the aoul by a gallant array of horsemen singing in full chorus their war songs; with perhaps a wandering minstrel to chant the praises of some hero; and it may be an astrologer or soothsayer to predict a happy termination to the journey of the guest they speed on his way. With equal comfort, if with less ceremony, is entertained the humbler traveller, who is entitled to ask shoes for his feet and a coat to his back of any man who has a supply of these necessaries; while a party of warriors on their journey may demand no less freely a kid from the flock or an ox from the herd. For there are three virtues, says a Circassian proverb, either one of which entitles the possessor to celebrity — bravery, eloquence, or hospitality — more literally, a sharp sword, a sweet tongue, or forty tables.

Though females are bought and sold in Circassia, and are deemed rather the helpmates than the companions of man, a chivalrous regard for the sex characterizes this race of warriors; and in no nation perhaps is woman in circumstances of exposure more certain of receiving respectful treatment. The warrior may place his arms around the neck of the maiden and let its steel-clad burden weigh gracefully upon her shoulders, but the familiarity which is modestly allowed as if it were that of a father or a brother does not degenerate into insult. And when the fair girl has once won this violently beating heart, and becomes the warrior's bride, she turns as coy as a western damsel in her teens. After marriage the fading of her early maidenly beauty is concealed as much as possible from the uxorious eye; in her white mantle her form is always graceful; by the evening fireside her presence never ceases to be a natural ornament and charm; and thus is kept up through a period of years, in the absence of confidential social intercourse, at least a certain portion of the illusion of first love.

But the principal characteristic of the manners of the Circassian warrior consists in his graceful, manly air and bearing. A strong sense of personal independence, of superiority even, is expressed in his looks, motions, and attitudes. Conscious of physical energy and bravery of soul, he has ever the self-possessed air of a man who knows no fear. The chivalrous sentiments of war fire his eye, distend his breast, and give erectness to his figure. His tread is as light as that of an Apollo; his repose as stately as that of an Aristides. Indeed it could not be otherwise than that there should be a native grace and dignity in the port of such lovers of liberty and their country as, for example, Mansur Bey, who said, "While the soul is in my mouth this country shall never be given to the Russian; when I die, I can no longer help it." The Circassian chieftain's blunt honesty and simple love of truth, his freedom from sordid selfishness and detestation of unmanly indulgences, give to his manners that stamp of heroism which all men admire in a Sickingen or a Cid. Even his vices, his hatred of an enemy, his contempt for a foreigner, his jealousy of rivals, his implacable love of revenge, have in them a dash of barbaric greatness, and nothing of the petty meanness of the vices of civilization and the times of peace.

XXV.

HIS PREDECESSORS.—MAHOMET-MOLLAH.

It was several years after Schamyl had taken his place in society as a warrior of full age, that his name first appeared in the annals of the Circassian war of independence. This was in connection with the siege of Himri, where he served as murid or disciple under the chieftain Khasi-Mollah.

This leader sprang up about the year 1830, and commenced a war of resistance to Russian encroachment in the eastern Caucasus, which was destined greatly to exceed in importance that which since the treaty of Adrianople had been waged by the Circassians proper in the western. For the latter contest, though a gallant and a successful one, has not down to the present time amounted to more than a guerilla, often interrupted by long intervals of quiet, and never prosecuted with any regularity of plan or permanent union of forces.

In the eastern Caucasus the flame of the war which has now been raging for a quarter of a century, was originally kindled at the torch of religious fanaticism. For Khasi-Mollah was a disciple of one Mahomet-Mollah, who was a cadi in the aoul of Jarach, in the khanate of Kurin, and who was reputed to be the wisest alim or teacher of Mahometan righteousness in the territory of Daghistan. The patriotic heart of this learned doctor had long been burning within him when, in the year 1823, he was induced, through the representations of one of his former pupils, to make a visit to another holy man in Schirwan, Hadis-Ismail by name, who expounded the Sufite doctrine to him more fully, and made a practical application of it to the political condition of his countrymen.

"Of what use," said finally Hadis-Ismail to Mahomet-Mollah, "is our going through the prescribed routine of prayers, our exact performance of ablutions, our adherence to the letter of the Scharyat, while the Sufis daily curse the followers of Omar? Let all true believers no longer contend against each other, but against the infidels. Campaigns to drive back the Muscovite are better than pilgrimages to worship at Kerbelah, and prayers to Allah are an abomination unless followed by a call to arms."

These were the words which Mahomet-Mollah had been waiting for years to hear spoken; and returning to Jarach he openly preached a crusade in behalf of freedom and the true faith. Immediately the report of this calling of all believers to arms against the Giaours spread like wildfire through Daghestan and the country of the Lesghians. Disciples came from afar to hear the new doctrine; and catching a portion of the fanatical zeal of the murschid, who enforced his views by depicting the barbarities then recently committed by the Russians in the neighboring district of Kara-Kaitach, they carried his burning words from aoul to aoul until the fury of the people burst out in a general rising to repel the advance of the invaders.

At this period the greater part of Daghestan, a territory lying on the Caspian, and eastward from the Lesghian highlands, had been brought under the yoke of the Russians. General Jermoloff, then governor-general of the Caucasus, had been very successful in extending the imperial dominion and influence, being himself no less a hero than the Circassian chieftains, possessing a noble form, a soul of bravery, hardy, persevering, and chivalrous. He secured by his gentle treatment the respect of those tribes which submitted to his rule, and by his ruthless severity made a terrible example of those who refused to do so. Going in advance of his arms, his intrigue penetrated into the fastnesses of the mountaineers, and taking advantage of the mutual jealousy of the tribes, fanning the hate of private feuds, widening the breach between the two hostile religious sects, and tempting all the chiefs by the promise of imperial honors, the people by the offer of free trade at the forts and market towns, it succeeded in gradually preparing the way for the advent of Russian intervention and authority with force of arms throughout all the less mountainous portions of Daghestan.

When, then, the active and sagacious governor heard that Mahomet-Mollah was preaching in Jarach a holy war against the Muscovites, and that he had erected in his house an altar before which the murids who came in from all the neighboring parts hourly prayed and said, "Moslem! war against the infidel! war against the infidel! death to the Giaour!" he sent a request to Arslan, khan of the Kasi-Kumucks, in whose territory was Jarach, that he should seize upon the person of the mollah. But Arslan, fearing to lay violent hands upon a teacher so venerated by the people, suffered him to escape into the adjacent territory of Avaria. There he lived until the recall of General Jermoloff permitted him to return to his native district; having meanwhile diligently called upon all believers to forget their sectarian differences, upon the members of the different tribes to lay aside their animosities, and upon all lovers of their country to rise in arms and drive back the infidel dogs who had dared invade the sanctity of the mountains.

"The first great law of our prophet," said he to the people, "is a law of freedom. No

Moslem shall be a slave, much less shall he acknowledge the rule of the foreigner and the unbeliever. And the second law is like unto the first. The Moslem shall be a soldier of Allah and his prophet, an enemy in arms of all infidels. For whosoever will not leave house, wife, and child, yea all that he hath or hopeth for to draw the sword for his faith, he shall not pass over the bridge El-Sirat into paradise. The Moslem shall keep the scharyat; but all his giving of alms to the poor, all his prayers and ablutions, all his pilgrimages to Mecca are nothing so long as the eye of a Muscovite looks upon them. Yea, your marriages are unlawful and your children bastards while there is a Muscovite in your midst. For who can serve both Allah and the Russian!"

XXVI.

KHASI-MOLLAH.

AMONG the murids of Mahomet-Mollah the foremost was Khasi-Mahomet, better known as Khasi-Mollah. After having spent much time sitting at the feet of the patriotic and fanatical murschid, he returned to his native aoul of Himri, and began his career as leader of the popular movement against Russia by sending to the neighboring tribes missives full of such reproof and exhortation as he had been in the habit of hearing at Jarach. This he continued to do until it became manifest that the time for decisive action had arrived, when accompanied by a considerable body of disciples, among whom was Schamyl, he sallied forth on an expedition of proselytism, and made his way first to the powerful aoul of Tcherkei, situated lower down on the Koissu, and in the territory of the Tchetchenians.

Assembling the warriors in a council ring, Khasi-Mollah said sharply to them, "Ye men of Tcherkei, ye are too much inclined to evil doing. Ye are guilty of idleness, of lying, of deceit, even as are others. The Christians have their gospel, the Jews their talmud, and we the koran; but in what are we better than others while we keep not the holy scharyat? There is but one path for us to paradise — it is the war path. Death to the Muscovites, and to all who are with them! Hate and war against the red-haired dogs, the unbelievers!"

Thereupon rose up an aged man of Tcherkei and said in reply, "Preach to us the scharyat; and we will obey it. We will cease from hating and robbing, and from all the sins you truly lay to our charge. But the Russians hold our chief men as hostages in Andrejewa; our herds are pastured in valleys subject to them; we are hemmed in on all sides by their strong places; every attempt we make to shake off their yoke only brings down on our heads retribution; and we cannot fight."

"Bide your time," rejoined Khasi-Mollah; "only be ready when I call; the day of your deliverance is at hand."

Then having received from the people a solemn promise that they would observe the scharyat, confirmed by a pouring out upon the ground of all the wine laid by in the aoul, as well as by the breaking of the wine vessels, he continued on his journey. Aoul after aoul was visited. Where persuasion failed, threats of fire and sword were resorted to; and in many instances promises of adherence were guaranteed by hostages sent to Himri. And so by dint of argument, intimidation, and force, the new doctrine of political Sufism was in the course of a few months diffused over the greater part of the Lesghian highlands.

Here and there, however, the more aged ulema* rejected the teaching that the taking up of arms against the infidels was the best fulfilment of the law of the scharyat, as for example in Chunsach, the principal aoul of

* Plural of alim.

Avaria, where, owing to strong Russian influence, the view prevailed that it was not expedient to run the risk of losing what of liberty was left by vainly attempting to regain that which had been lost. Accordingly Pachu Biké, who here bore rule under the title of Khaness, prayed Khasi-Mollah not to enter the Avarian territory; but he persisting, she called together her warriors to resist him. They, however, fearing at first to face the determined band of murids, she seized a sword and cried out, "Go home, ye men of Chunsach, and gird on your wives the swords ye are unworthy to bear yourselves!" Thereupon the warriors, stung with shame, followed the amazon who immediately put herself at their head and drove back Khasi-Mollah, though supported by a force of eight thousand men.

This repulse turned the hearts of many of the recently converted away from the new prophet; so that when in the summer of 1830, General Von Rosen, who had taken the command of the army after the brief and inefficient career in the Caucasus of Paskievitch, the successor of Jermoloff, marched on Himri to crush the germ of war which was preparing to unfold itself in this part of the mountains, the chief men of the neighboring aouls hastened in great numbers to give in their adhesion to the supremacy of the Russians. So general in fact was the appearance of submission that Von Rosen, staying his advance, let Himri go unpunished.

"The enemy are smitten by Allah with blindness!" exclaimed Khasi-Mollah as he heard that the Russians were retracing their footsteps without penetrating further into the mountains. "They could not see their advantage. As is written in the book of the prophet, 'With blindness will I smite them!'"

This interpretation of the turning back of Von Rosen, struck the heated imaginations of the mountaineers with such force that they all regarded it as a miraculous interposition of Allah in behalf of the new prophet; and when Khasi-Mollah, taking advantage of this sudden turn of men's minds towards him, defeated a detachment sent under Prince Bekovitsch to disperse a gathering of murids in the woods of Tchunkeskan, his fame increased in the land, and a large number of warriors flocked around his standard.

The next year, therefore, he was enabled to perform the great feat of capturing Tarku, an important place on the Caspian, and of laying siege to the fortress of Burnaja which overlooks it. The reinforcements of the enemy compelled him indeed to retire; but not until after several days of desperate fighting, and when he had literally strewn the streets of Tarku with his dead. Then devastating the unfriendly aouls on the Sulak, beating General Emanuel in a pitched battle, converting by fire and sword the district of Tabasseran which had held with the Russians, blockading the strong town of Derbend until it was relieved by superior numbers, and storming Kisliar on the Terek whence he carried away captives and much treasure, he terminated the conquests of the season by captivating the heart of a daughter of Mahomet-Mollah, whom he took to wife, and then retired into winter quarters in Himri.

Shortly before he had issued the following call, written in Arabic, to the tribes of Daghestan:—

"Hear all ye men of Daghestan! Our next breaking into the territory of the unfriendly tribes will be like the rising red of the morning. Blood will mark our track; fire and desolation will be left behind us; and what words cannot describe shall be executed in deeds. But accept the new doctrine and your lives shall be spared, and your property left in your possession. The song of the nightingale in the spring will be the sign of our coming. So soon as the snow melts on the mountains, and the new year puts on its green, we shall sweep over the hostile aouls, taking by force what is denied to forbearance. We are the terror of the unbelieving, but the strength and refuge of the faithful; and he who follows us shall have peace and eternal life. Amen."

But in Himri was destined to terminate the brief career of glory run by Khasi-Mollah. With the first singing of birds he did indeed go forth, carrying devastation beyond the Russian lines, even from Kisliar to Wladikaukas, from the Caspian to the central Caucasus; but the Russian commander-in-chief, accompanied by General Williaminoff, Prince Dadian, and the valiant Austrian Kluke Von Klugenau, forced the prophet to retire and take refuge behind the triple walls of Himri. Thereupon, during the retreat, the warriors who had been compelled to join his standard contrary to their inclination, gradually fell off; one by one the chieftains deserted him as they saw the superiority of the forces of the enemy; even the principal murid, Hamsad Bey, deceived, it is said, by forged proclamations issued in the name of the prophet, separated himself from a leader whose fortunes were so evidently on the wane; and when October's unfallen leaves were still covering the hills of Himri, the Russian bayonets arrived to add their gleam to the gorgeousness of the autumnal decay of nature.

There was now no escape for the faithful few who still adhered to the cause of Khasi-Mollah, among whom was Schamyl. The artillery under the direction of General Williaminoff soon brought down the towers of loose stones over the devoted heads of the murids in Himri. But they met their fate chanting verses from the Koran. No man had a thought of surrender, though the paths into the mountains were all in the possession of the enemy. From street to street and from house to house fought the men of Himri. Their granite rocks were as red with blood as the leaves of the trees with the glory of the autumn. Khasi-Mollah, though from his priestly character he did not himself bear arms, fell surrounded by the dead bodies of sixty of his disciples. Schamyl also lay at his feet bored through by two balls, and was left there by the enemy for dead. When the Russians found the corpse of Khasi-Mollah, the right hand still pointed to heaven, the left grasped the beard, and over the face was spread the placid expression of a dream instead of the last agony.

Khasi-Mollah was of a short stature, with small eyes, a thin, long beard, and a countenance somewhat marked by smallpox.

XXVII.

HAMSAD BEY.

The manner of Schamyl's escape and recovery from the wounds received at Himri never having been explained by himself, was believed by the mountaineers to have been miraculous. Certain it is he survived to receive the mantle of the heroic Khasi-Mollah, though in descending to him it rested for a short time on the shoulders of Hamsad Bey.

This leader possessed neither the fanatical zeal of his predecessor nor the military genius of the still greater prophet who came after him; but being consecrated by Mahomet-Mollah as the successor of Khasi-Mollah, notwithstanding his separation from the latter previously to the fight at Himri, he was universally acknowledged as the chief of the new party. The first of the two years of his rule was spent by him in making preparations for taking the field, during which time he had the address to gather together a considerable number of Russian deserters whom he formed into a separate corps commanded by their own officers, and in whom, being attached to him by good treatment, he placed such entire confidence that he even made them his body-guard. This was something new in the annals of Circassian warfare; but it was an innovation of short duration and very questionable utility, inasmuch as such a perfect machine as the Russian soldier could work to little advantage by the side of the Circassian warrior with his impetuous impulses and action independent of the word of command.

The only feat of arms attempted during this year by Hamsad Bey was a successful attack on the aoul of Chergow, in the Mechtulinian district; but the spring following he concentrated his forces, amounting to some twelve thousand men, in the aoul of Gotsatl, in Avaria, eighteen wersts east of Chunsach, for the purpose of striking a blow at Russian ascendency in the neighboring districts of Daghestan. But to do this effectually it was necessary first to put an end to the influence of the enemy in Avaria itself, and to substitute his own spiritual authority as murschid in place of the deference paid there to the hereditary khans.

Accordingly Hamsad Bey marched on Chunsach, where Pachu Biké with her three sons held for the Muscovites. Pitching his tent before this populous aoul, he sent in his herald to the khaness requiring her to adopt the new religion of hatred against the Russians, and to join her forces with his to drive them out of the country. Pachu Biké, who had so heroically taken up arms against Khasi-Mollah, now thought it more prudent to try the fortune of negotiation, and for that purpose sent her two eldest sons, Omar Khan and Abu-Nunzal, to treat with the murschid. But the latter having got the princes in his possession, caused them to be put to death; then followed up his treachery by seizing upon the unresisting aoul; and having decapitated the khaness herself, destroyed all of the reigning race save her youngest son Bulatsch

Khan, a lad eleven years of age, who was then not present in Chunsach.

The submission of all Avaria, together with several adjacent districts, followed these acts of barbarous severity on the part of Hamsad Bey; but the avenger of blood followed close behind him. Two brothers, Osman and Hadji-Murad, being foster-brothers of Omar Khan, resolved to satisfy the law which requires in Circassia, as formerly in Judea, that whosoever sheddeth man's blood, by man shall his blood be shed. They were at the time murids of Hamsad Bey, but being urged on by their father, a man venerable in years, and opposed to the reformed party in religion, they were induced to set their allegiance to the law of vengeance before their loyalty to their chief, and accordingly conspired to take him off. Forty of their relations and friends joined the conspiracy, all taking an oath on the Koran to be faithful to each other, and never to rest until they had slain Hamsad Bey. But one among them proved to be a traitor. Going straightway to the murschid he revealed the plot of the two brothers. But the Bey, confiding in the loyalty of disciples who had given him so many proofs of fidelity, would not listen to the tale, and peacefully resumed the sleep from which he had been awakened to hear it.

On the morrow he fell dead in the mosque of Chunsach, pierced by the pistol balls of the two murids. One of them, Osman, instantly received the reward of his treachery in the loss of his life at the hands of the attendants of the prophet; but the other, Hadji-Murad, escaping in the confusion of the moment, brought the crowd outside to his assistance by raising the cry of, "Down with the murids." With sabre and pistol they rushed into the house of Allah, and in a moment all its stones were red with the blood of his children. Only thirty out of the one hundred murids of Hamsad Bey escaped from the mosque with their lives. These flying before the excited multitude sought refuge in the neighboring tower; but this being built of wood was set on fire by the order of Hadji-Murad. Then of the thirty, some precipitated themselves headlong from the top of the tower; others fell fighting; Mahomet-Hadshi-Jaf, the same who had betrayed the conspirators, being sorely wounded was taken captive; only one escaped, as if by miracle — it was Schamyl.

XXVIII.

CIRCASSIAN MODE OF WARFARE.

SUCH were the leaders under whom Schamyl served his apprenticeship in the art of war. But from his youth up he had also been trained for the great military part he was to play in life by engaging in those raids and forays by means of which the Circassians were wont at that period to harass and keep at bay the enemy. For while from lack of unanimity among the tribes, from want of a hero like Schamyl to lead them, from the superiority of the Russian forces, or from whatever other cause, the mountaineers were engaged in no great, combined movements of self-defence, there was notwithstanding constantly kept up, by most of the tribes of both the eastern and the western Caucasus, the running fire of the guerilla, and the predatory expeditions of a war of the border.

Such expeditions were set on foot either by some chieftain who rode from aoul to aoul calling upon the brave to follow him; or by a summons sent abroad to the warriors of a certain district inviting them to assemble in the council ring at a given time and place for the purpose of agreeing upon an attack upon some fort, or a foray within the lines of the enemy. The spot selected for holding the assembly would be some convenient hill-top or vale shaded by trees. There, with no little rude eloquence, accompanied by the singing the praises of heroes, the subject of the proposed expedition would be considered, and the course to be pursued be determined by a majority of voices. With scarcely the formality of an election, the general preference would select some chieftain to head the incursion, if finally agreed upon. And to set off, if the occasion pressed, would hardly require more preparation than the springing into their saddles; for at the bows of these could quickly be hung a sufficiency of provisions for their simple wants, while ammunition and arms are always worn about their person.

The Circassian spares his horse when he can, and generally rides slowly to the scene of contest. Indeed, the route admits of no hurrying; for it often leads along precipices which would turn almost any head but his own; winds a narrow, rugged path over the mountains; picks its way along the rocky bed of the torrent; dives into forests tangled with vines and brambles; and cannot always turn aside even from the bog and the quagmire. But his hardy steed never tires; and up hill or down dale toils patiently, bravely, cheerfully, as if conscious that he was going on to meet the armed men, and smelling afar off the future battle, the thunder of the captains, and the shouting. Sometimes the party travels through the night, each warrior being muffled in a shaggy capote or bourka, which covers not only the rider but the entire back of his steed. Above protrude the barrels of the rifles, while below dangle the horse-tails, making, by their constantly dangling to and fro, the night-march a very promenade of hobgoblins.

But on the longer expeditions the war party halts at night. Some green spot having been selected where there is pasturage and water, the horses are tethered, or allowed to graze under care of persons appointed to watch them. Their saddles furnish a pillow at night, and their cloth a carpet to sit upon. Each person contributes from the leathern bottles and bags at his saddle-bow a portion towards the general mess, which is prepared by a certain number of the party in turn; and while it is being made ready, the others having said their evening prayers and performed their ablutions resign themselves to the soothing influences of the chibouque, if not prohibited, and to the cordial of coffee, if they have any. The supper at the very best will consist of hot millet or barley cakes, and the savory pilaff of minced mutton and millet or rice. A little honey will be sure to be added, and possibly dried fruits. This, however, is on the supposition that there are a few sumpter horses loaded with provisions, as is generally the case when the party is a large one. There may also have been more or less game picked up by the way. A bowl of mead or *skhone* is generally to be had by the Circassian, let the supper it accompanies be never so scanty; and the sharp appetite which heaven sends to those journeying through the hills in the saddle, will season even a little sour milk and a few cakes of millet and honey, if there be nothing else, with more than the savor of a feast. The chieftain fares no better than his clansmen; all share in the mess alike.

The supper finished, and every man having carefully cleansed his weapons, loaded and primed his guns and pistols, placed his sabre by his saddle-pillow, while his faithful poniard guards the side it never leaves, and finally a short prayer for protection having been offered to Allah, the sentinels also being duly set, the warrior who is to fall in battle on the morrow lies down to sleep as peaceful as that of the babe he has left behind in the aoul, and soft as if the canopy overhead were not the star-spangled curtain of the skies. If the party have tents, as is sometimes the case, they are pitched by cutting down branches of trees for lack of poles, and then covering them with the mats and felts which have been transported in bales on horseback. These simple structures serve sufficiently well to keep out wind and rain; while the boughs of many kinds of trees furnish a couch both elastic and fragrant.

Watch fires, too, are often kept burning through the night; and in cold weather they serve likewise to keep warm those sleeping around them. When the fires are numerous they light up with picturesque effect the grim-faced rocks and the solemn woods. A whole mountain side even may be illuminated by the multitude of flames, making the granite, porphyry, and limestone glow with colors more gorgeous than those borrowed from the light of day. Or the gloom of the deep glen is dissipated and devoured by the lambent tongues of fire, while the rocks over against each other burn with the additional radiance reflected from their faces. Beacon answers to beacon from cliffs and hill-tops. Perhaps the enemy's fires far off diffuse a glow through another quarter of the heavens. The reeds of the Kuban and the Terek set on fire by the Russians to destroy the ambuscades of the mountaineers, touch with a dull red tint the low northern horizon; here and there conflagrations raging in the grass-grown steppes show at night where lie the vast and dreary confines of the Muscovite; while perhaps the moon sinking below the Black mountains draws, with a line of silver, the broken outline of their ridges, leaving in the blackness of midnight the vast forests and outcropping rocks below.

When the first faint blush of breaking day suffuses the eastern sky far off above the Caspian, the warrior's eye already open is straining to catch it. His tent is struck; his horse saddled; his arms girded on; and he ready for the march. As the gray dawn deepening to crimson fills the mountains ere the sun be risen with its increasing, all-pervading light, the horsemen descend in small parties from the already purple heights into the mists which hang their thin veils over the depths of the valleys. Their arms reflect the beams of the risen sun, and the red or purple in their caps is heightened by the glow of the mountain tops. Gaily they gallop down the easy declivities, their horses snuffing eagerly the fresh air of the morning, but their ragged banners too wet with the dews of night to flaunt upon the zephyrs that, newly risen, scarcely move their wings. The foremost riders, gaining the open valley screened by an intervening mountain from the plain of the enemy, prance over it, and companies of horse coming in from different directions join the general rendezvous until, all counted, they may amount to two or three hundred, or as many thousand men. For seldom does a Circassian chief lead on a raid into the enemy's country with either less than the former number or more than the latter.

The guides now come in from reconnoitring the posture of affairs on the steppe on the other side of the mountain. In accordance with their advice most probably had the expedition been originally agreed upon; for they had represented the enemy's flocks and herds as left unguarded save by the shepherds, the villages undefended except by the boors, and the posture of things generally to be such as to promise a certain victory with booty and captives. Now they come in, having taken a final survey from some wooded nook on the hill-side of the boundless steppean prospect, as from his cottage on the cliff the fisherman looks out upon the level waste of the ocean. The Terek is reported sufficiently low to be forded; for the stream which in the higher mountains pours down with headlong fury its waters, transparent save where the white and red crystals which form its bed are concealed by the foam, creeps through the steppe a sluggish, muddy current, passable with safety at certain points and certain stages of the water. In the plain beyond stands a Cossack village or stanitza, together with a small fort or krepost surrounded by mud walls, armed with a piece or two of artillery, and garrisoned by a small body of infantry. It is one of the chain of similar Cossack settlements which, called "the line" of the Caucasus, stretches from the mouth of the Kuban to that of the Terek; and as the invaders penetrate further and further into the mountains, they carry this system of Cossack colonies and fort defenses with them, so that the chain forged to bind within its thousand links the liberties of all the tribes is gradually drawn tighter and tighter.

Over against the ford, and at no great distance from it, stands a Cossack guard-post. It is constructed of four poles twenty or more feet in height, which below are fastened in the earth and support on the upper extremity a seat or lookout. To this the Cossack climbs by means of a ladder, and there he sits by day and by night watching the forest of reeds on the river banks, watching the level sweep of the steppe on either side, watching the opposite hills and mountains. Forlorn indeed would be the poor Cossack notwithstanding he has before his eyes the glory of the Circassian hills and the distant snow-summits mingling with the clouds, were it not for the bottle of schnapps by his side, and the stroking of his long moustache. For weeks and months he may watch without seeing a single Circassian. But when he does, he instantly kindles his beacon fire, and descending seizes his lance left leaning against one of the four posts, and springing upon his horse which stands fastened to another, gallops to the stanitza. In all haste the women and children fly to the fort; the soldiers drive in the swine or cattle which feed on the grass around it; the sentinels fire the cannon to give the alarm to the neighboring stanitzas; and every Cossack within sound of the signal-firing, vaulting into the saddle and putting his steed to his mettle, hastens lance in hand to drive back the enemy.

But ere he arrives, though fleet be his steed, very likely the Circassian band, having previously succeeded in reaching the river unobserved, have swept like a tempest over both fort and stanitza. An oath of fidelity which even more than any divinity awes the Circassian mind and rules it, having previously been administered on a pocket edition of the Koran to each warrior by his chief, and each one before sallying from his place of concealment in reeds, woods, or hills, having dismounted to put up with raised hands in silence a brief prayer to Allah, as well as to tighten his saddle-girths, at a given signal all spring forward like the roused lion out of his lair. Giving their horses the rein they have no need of spurs. In a moment they are across the open space which lies between their cover and the fortress, though some may have fallen from the enemy's well-aimed guns and musketry. They are at the gates; they leap the ditch;

they climb the wall; they spring down into the enclosure; at the same time raising a war-cry which resembling the shrill, melancholy, and fearfully wild howl of the jackal, fills with unnatural, and even insane consternation the troops who for the first time hear it. It is now quick work, and the struggle fearful. But the agile and light-limbed mountaineers are more than a match for the heavy, slow-witted Russians; and though in cold blood the former do not take the life of an enemy, now fury-driven they are swift to smite and never spare; while above the clash of sabres and bayonets, above the shouting and the musketry, rises the voice of the Circassian chief who leads on and deals out destruction until the last Muscovite bites the dust.

The stanitza making no resistance, the work of pillage is soon done; whereupon the troop having picked up their dead and wounded, turn their horses' heads again towards the mountains. When the Cossacks come in with their reinforcements it is too late. They are only in time to behold the stanitza in flames, the fort in ruins from the explosion of its magazines, and the victors, their cruppers piled high with goods, and women, just gaining the opposite bank, or crossing the hill-top, on the other side of which lie both safety and freedom.

Sometimes the Circassians dash through between the forts without stopping to attack them, and suffering, perhaps, somewhat from the cross-fire, gain the country beyond the line, where they find more abundant spoils and no resistance. But on their return, they are sure to encounter the Cossacks drawn up at the ford, or some other point convenient for disputing the passage to an enemy encumbered with booty. These Russian hirelings, however, the freemen of the mountains despise, and with superior horses ride them down. Only when the espionage which is maintained among all the tribes on the border — for everywhere there are souls which can be bought for gold — succeeds in procuring for their enemies information of any incursion before it takes place, is the foray rendered unsuccessful and the troop cut off.

XXIX.

RUSSIAN MODE OF WARFARE.

The Russian mode of conducting the invasion of the Caucasus has been different at different times. When the Emperor Nicholas, after the treaty of Adrianople in 1829, revived the old war with Circassia in order to compel by force of arms the acknowledgment of those pretended rights of supremacy which by that treaty had been made over to him by Turkey, he supposed that his Cossacks, aided by a small force of infantry, would be sufficient to intimidate the mountaineers and to accomplish his purpose. Earlier in the century, Russia had acquired from Persia the vast provinces of the southern Caucasus, and had afterwards, partly by the consent of the tribes and partly by force, succeeded in keeping open the two great routes to these possessions, the one along the Caspian, and the other over the centre of the chain by the pass of Dariel. It remained therefore to subjugate only that portion of the Caucasus not included in the territories adjacent to these two roads, and lying the larger portion of it south of the Kuban, and the smaller south of the Terek.

Nicholas accordingly sent his proclamations into the mountains saying, "Russia has conquered France, put her sons to death, and made captives of her daughters. England will never give any aid to the Circassians, because she depends on Russia for her daily bread. There are only two powers in the universe — God in heaven, and the emperor on earth! What then do you expect? Even though the arch of heaven were to fall, there are Russians enough to hold it up on the points of their bayonets!" At the same time, while the Cossack colonies which had been planted in line along the northern banks of the Kuban and the Terek were reinforced from the hordes of their brethren on the Black Sea and the Don, the long spears of these united horsemen were strengthened by the bayonets of a few thousand infantry — the vanguard of hundreds of thousands who were to come after them.

But the Circassians heard with incredulous ears the big words of the lieutenants of the czar. They knew not, besides, why he should pretend to rule over them. The Turks had indeed enjoyed the privilege of establishing fortified places of trade on their coasts, and as most of the tribes had been converted from paganism by Mahometan missionaries, they looked upon the sultan as their spiritual head and Allah's vicegerent, but they did not consider their free mountains as in any sense his domain, nor liable by any treaty stipulations to be transferred to another superior, much less to the unbelieving Padischah of the "flax-haired Christian dogs," and their old enemies, the Muscovites. Accordingly, like true and independent men and the sons of sires who without let or hinderance had pastured their flocks in these mountains since the days of the patriarchs, they refused to give up the ancient freedom of their homes, built on the rocks, at the bidding of the minions of the autocrat of the North.

The Cossacks who came galloping across the steppes on small, shaggy horses, and armed with unwieldly lances, the mountaineers looked upon with contempt. They sabred them and rode them down. As for the Russian infantry, they were terror-struck at the sound of the yell with which these centaurs of the mountains dashed into the thickest of their ranks, shooting them down with pistols, striking back their bayonets with their sabres, leaping from their saddles to poniard them, and the next instant gone on a gallop with the wind. The soldier who had been at the retreat from Moscow, and at the crossing of the Borodino, and who was a good and true grenadier, sturdy, brave, obedient to the word of command, felt all his forces desert him before the onset of such reckless riders and accomplished swordsmen. Once across the Kuban or the Terek, he never felt sure of his life, for there was always a Circassian lying in wait for him. When the column was wending its way through the narrow valley wherein nature held her supreme and silent reign, save that the tiny brook ran with gurgling sounds over its rocks and pebbles, or the nightingale made the thickets vocal with its song, or the bees flitting from flower to flower diffused through the air a pleasing murmur, wherein the oak spread its peaceful branches against the sky, the beech leaning over the path shed a grateful shade, and the vine hanging in festoons from elm to maple invited the weary soldier to refresh his lips with their purple clusters, there lay hid in this sweet solitude a hundred men and more armed for battle; and when the invaders no more suspected danger from the peaceful hill-sides than the bird from the snare of the fowler,

> Instant, through copse and heath arose
> Bonnets and spears and bended bows;
> On right, on left, above, below,
> Sprung up at once the lurking foe.

Then instead of the singing of the brook, the carol of the nightingale, and the humming of the sweet-mouthed bees, were heard the rifle's sharp crack and the rattling of the musketry; the brook ran red with the blood of the slain; and the Russians, like the Roman legions cut off in the woods of the Germans, were left with none to bury them.

Nor even within the walls of the forts was the Russian soldier entirely safe from his wily adversary. For when silently beneath the moon the sentry is pacing the narrow rounds of the krepost, suspecting no enemy within a dozen leagues, but thinking rather of the hut on Polish plains or shores of Finnish lake fondly called a home, some Adighé or Lesghian who, unable to rest until he has slaked his thirst for vengeance in the blood of an infidel, has stolen down from the mountains and lain hid a day in the reeds of the river bank, creeps at nightfall like a wild beast out of his lair, glides unseen by the guard-post of the Cossack as the latter is taking perhaps a final pull at his bottle of schnapps, and crawling up within sight of the very beard of the sentinel, picks him off.

Accordingly the army of the emperor, instead of making an easy conquest of the Caucasus, was obliged to remain for the most part shut up in the chain of their miserable forts and kreposts. Here, when these fortified places were not boldly assaulted and carried by storm, as often happened, the troops fell a gradual prey to fevers and dysenteries, or to the want of those supplies which the peculation of the officers in charge of them continually either withheld or adulterated. The forts, situated on the coast of the Black Sea, could be relieved only during that half of the year which was suited for navigation; while those on the Kuban and the Terek were dependent on the precarious supplies conveyed overland at such times as the roads were passable. To keep up the spirits of the imprisoned garrisons the men were made to sing by word of command; and the dance was introduced as a military exercise. The Caucasus in fact became a southern Siberia, where the average life of the soldier was but three years.

Taught at length by repeated and disastrous failures that this method of attacking the Circassians was a fatal error, the czar next adopted the plan of sending into the mountains heavy masses of infantry supported by powerful trains of field artillery. These with great labor penetrated a certain distance into the interior for the purpose of opening roads from one important fortress to another, and guarding them with chains of mud forts or kreposts. They made reconnoissances in various directions, succeeded in isolating and subduing some of the districts lying on the Kuban and Laba rivers, and completed the subjugation of the more open country of the Kabardan tribes, who were obliged to accept terms of neutrality.

At the same time the invaders adopted the additional plan of blockading the mountains both by sea and land. Besides the line of fortresses commenced by Peter the Great on the Terek, extended by Catherine westward, and now completed from sea to sea, similar establishments were created on all the points of the Black Sea coast which could conveniently be approached by water. Under pretence of carrying out a rigid system of quarantine regulations and tariff laws, the object was to cut off the Circassians from all foreign intercourse, and especially from trade with the Turks, who were in the habit of supplying them with arms, gunpowder, salt, and various necessary articles of manufacture. At the same time, the Russians endeavored by making certain marts of their own free to the mountaineers, to induce them gradually to exchange the habits of war for those of trade and friendly intercourse with their adversaries. Emissaries were sent among the tribes to attempt to win them over to this change of policy; rank in the army was offered to the chiefs; or they were tempted by pensions; and even by the introduction of foreign brandy as well as foreign gold, efforts were made to spread the fatal net of Russian influence along all the footpaths of freedom in the mountains.

The Circassians liked the taste of the foreign liquor, and their eyes were not insensible to the charms of coined gold, of which they had before seen but little. The epaulettes also and stars and ribands were such baubles as were well adapted to captivate the fancy of semi-civilized chieftains; and the Russian fabrics were a temptation to all, especially to the women; but to the honor of the Circassians, the tribes with few exceptions disdained to sell their birthright of independence for a mere mess of pottage. Relations of trade and amity could be established only with the tribes whose position on the frontier compelled them to be neutral. The chiefs in the interior, though often jealous of each other, held themselves too high to be bought by the common enemy for a price; and the intrigue of the czar was on the whole as unsuccessful as his arms.

The Circassians at first made little or no change in their mode of warfare to meet the new tactics of the invader. Still despising the men who dwelt in plains notwithstanding their cannon "made the earth to tremble and the fruit drop from the trees," they continued from time to time to storm the kreposts sabre in hand. They leaped out of their places of ambush upon the columns which attempted to penetrate into their fastnesses; and attacking the more numerous enemy in dense masses as formerly practised by the Turkish spahis, setting all modern tactics at defiance, and bent on bearing down every thing before them by the mad fury of their onset, they rushed upon the Russian squares and guns as if they had been the mere branches of trees used in their own mock-fights.

For the most part they were victorious; but every victory cost them much precious blood, a fresh supply of which could not so easily be obtained as was the case with the viler sort which flowed in the veins of the imperial serfs and peasants. They were therefore obliged in the end to become less prodigal of it, and to adopt a system of guerilla warfare better adapted to the comparative fewness of their warriors and the extraordinary strength of their natural means of defence. To cut off convoys, to surprise outposts, to hover about the march of the enemy's columns, to lie in wait for them in the passes of the mountains, to pick off their officers from behind rocks and bushes, to attack in numbers only in cases of great moment and when the nature of the ground rendered a successful dash practicable before the straggling column could form square, and to undertake the storming of fortified places, and the plundering of hostile districts only when these were left comparatively defenceless, was finally the method of warfare which experience had forced upon the tribes at the period when Schamyl appeared on the scene as their leader.

XXX.

HIS PERSONAL APPEARANCE.

Schamyl was thirty-seven years of age when he was raised to the rank of a murschid and leader of the tribes. At that period in his prime, he had outgrown the early delicacy of his constitution, and was a warrior as distinguished in personal appearance as in character and intellectual culture. He was of middle stature; had fair hair, since turned to white; grey eyes overshadowed by thick, well-drawn brows; a mouth, like his hands and feet, small; a regular, so-called Grecian nose; and a complexion remarkable among his countrymen for its fairness and delicacy of skin. He had the light, elastic Circassian tread, with little movement of his arms in walking, an erect carriage, and a naturally noble air and bearing. Perfectly master of himself and of his countenance, sternly self-collected even in moments of the greatest danger, holding in perpetual balance the ardor of the warrior and the calm of the prophet, he impressed with awe all who came into his presence. As he regarded himself as an instrument in the hands of a higher power, and held according to the doctrine of the Sufis that all his thoughts and decisions were the immediate inspiration of Allah, so he condemned to death the traitor and conferred the shaska of honor on a murid with equal calmness, manifesting neither anger nor satisfaction, almost as impassive and impersonal as fate itself. But while his ordinary manner was thus calmly commanding, his eloquence was as fiery as it was persuasive. "Flames sparkle from his eyes," said Bersek Bey, "and flowers are scattered from his lips."

Schamyl is said to have put on a white mantle, indicative of his priestly character as the second prophet of Allah; but his ordinary dress and arms were the same as those in use, with trifling variations, among all Circassians.

They wear a surtout resembling a military Polonaise, without a collar, closely fitting the body, descending to the knees, and secured around the waist by a leathern girdle, which is ornamented according to the wealth or fancy of the wearer. On either breast of this garment are attached cartridge-pockets made of morocco leather of different colors, usually containing twenty-four rounds of ball cartridge, and at the same time decking the chest and protecting it. Beneath is a tunic, often richly embroidered, and of a gay color. The trousers are loose, excepting that from the ankle to the knee the folds are confined to the leg by straps. The calpac or cap has a crown similar in color to the cartridge-pockets, with a band of long, black goat's hair or white sheep's wool, which hanging down about the brows imparts a wild fierceness of expression to the dark, flashing eyes, and boldly cut features. Sometimes a chieftain will also wind around his cap a shawl in the form of a turban, his head being shaven after the manner of the Turks, though the tuft on the crown is generally much larger. The shoes are made of a single piece of leather, and neatly show the form of the foot. Under the other garments is worn a shirt of either silk or calico, besides that of mail sometimes put on in war; and over all is thrown in cold weather an ample cloak called a *bourka,* woven of sheep's wool or goat's hair, and impervious to rain.

This convenient and picturesque costume is also set off by much silver lace, embroidery, and all the elegant artifice of needle-work, but still more by the various arms without which no Circassian appears in public. A rifle is slung across the shoulders by a belt, this weapon having taken the place of the bow and arrows which are now seldom seen except as an ornament and mark of distinction. The sabre, called a shaska, is suspended by a silken cord in the Turkish fashion. In the girdle are stuck a pair of pistols, and a short, double-edged cama, resembling the sword of the ancient Romans. This latter arm in close conflicts with the Russian infantry is particularly dreaded from the dexterity with which it is wielded, a single stroke generally sufficing to sever a limb, while recovery from its stab is almost hopeless. Attached to the girdle also are a powder-flask, a small metallic box containing fat to anoint the rifle-balls, a purse of skin for carrying flints, tinder, and steel, and not unfrequently a hatchet, or knife in a sheath. The sabre is silver-hilted, without a guard; and its scabbard, richly embroidered, is composed of several pieces of morocco of different colors. The pistols also are mounted with silver; the poniard has often precious stones in its handle, and its sheath is inlaid with mother-of-pearl. Sometimes a javelin in addition to other arms is carried, which is hurled to a considerable distance with an aim that rarely errs. Having a groove at the but-end, it is used also as a rest for the rifle, besides serving as a pole in leaping among the rocks.

Coats of mail with casques of steel, cuirasses, cuisses, brassards, and gauntlets, formerly much used and worth from ten up to three hundred oxen, are now little esteemed; though chain armor, resembling that of the ancient Persians, is still worn occasionally by the chiefs of tribes. This is generally of considerable antiquity, exquisitely wrought, of perfect temper, light, elastic, and fitting the body closely. There are also still in use a good many swords, now diminished by use a third or more in width, which have come down from the Genevese, Venetians, Milanese, and Spaniards of the middle ages. Of these the Toledan blade is the most common; and travellers curious in antique arms have noted one possessing the genuine silvery lustre, and engraved with the picture of a Spanish cavalier, together with the motto, *Ad majorem gloriam Dei;* another which was dedicated to God, and marked, *Anno domini* 1664; another showing on one side an imperial crown, encircled by a wreath of laurel, and on the other a globe surmounted by a cross, with the inscription underneath in old English characters, *Viva Espagna;* and others, finally, inlaid with gold, and having the head of the Saviour, or some saint engraved over such inscriptions as, *Par my Dey y par my Rey*, or, *Ne me tire pas sans raison et ne me remets pas sans honneur.* Nor is the modern Circassian sabre one of metal inferior to that of the ancient workmanship; but a blade as flexible as that of Damascus, long and heavy, yet bending like a reed, and when inlaid and ornamented with gold valued as high as three hundred roubles, or even more.

The wealth of a Circassian consists very much in his arms and horses. It may even happen that a chieftain may wear a coat which is out at the elbows, and especially when going to battle,—for though he may fall himself he always thinks it a pity to waste a new doublet and hose upon "the dog of a Muscovite,"—and yet be the possessor of a balteus for his bow as richly jewelled as was Diana's, and a corytos in the superb style of the ancient Persians, as found represented on Persepolitan bas-reliefs. The trappings of his horse also may be made costly with Russian leather and chased silver ornaments. Nor in the case of a leader less illustrious than Schamyl even, would it be a thing impossible for his saddle to be covered with blue velvet, adorned with black enamelled silver plates, stirrups of massive silver, and bridle no less brilliantly ornamented, the work of the cunning artificers of Armenia.

In all these costly trappings of war does the Circassian leader take great delight, nor did Schamyl himself disdain them; and when fully arrayed in them, as on all festal occasions at least he is sure to be, with brawny shoulders and thin flank, a peculiarly airy, winged gait, a naturally unconstrained and noble air, a countenance displaying the highest type of manly beauty, and eyes passionate even to an intensity bordering upon fierceness, Murat was not a gayer horseman, Bayard not a better knight, nor is the Apollo Belvidere more like a god.

XXXI.

BECOMES IMAM, AND CONTINUES THE WAR.

AT the time of Hamsad Bey's death Mahomet-Mollah being no longer living to select and consecrate a new leader of the tribes, that Schamyl attained to the honors of the succession was very much owing to the exertions of his venerable teacher Dschelal Eddin. For the latter was then the most eminent murschid left in the eastern Caucasus, where his sayings passed current among a large number of the tribes as oracles. Schamyl's principal rival was Taschaw-Hadji, an influential chieftain who resisted the supremacy of the new Imam, as he was called, until the year 1837, when he formally gave in his adhesion. This opposition, however, while it lasted, considerably hindered the growth of Schamyl's influence among the tribes, and restrained the freedom of his action against the Russians. The emissaries of the latter meanwhile did all they could to fan the discord, so that several chiefs with their clans were either won over to the side of the common enemy, or were at least rendered unwilling to coöperate with the Imam in his efforts to extend the new faith and prosecute the war.

Of this Russian party in the highlands Avaria still remained the head-quarters; and during the first four years of Schamyl's imamship his aims were chiefly directed towards the subjugation of this district. Hadji-Murad, who after the assassination of the Avarian princes had continued at the head of affairs in Chunsach, early foresaw that this would be his policy. Accordingly he lost no time in sending to the Russian commander-in-chief a request that he would despatch an armed force to take possession in the name of the emperor of the khanate, then vacant by the death of the youngest son of Pachu Biké, who had been assassinated, as was said, by order of Schamyl.

Thereupon General Lasskoi being placed in command of a considerable body of troops, was ordered to march on Chunsach, and to sweep the country on his way of all opposition. Advancing accordingly in the autumn of 1834 against Himri, he captured the place after a slight resistance, its population having been greatly reduced since the defeat experienced there under Khasi-Mollah. But as the victor was about to proceed further on his march, Schamyl arrived with his murids, took the aoul by storm, and inflicted a severe loss upon the enemy, though greatly his superior in numbers. When, however, this news reached the fortress of Temir-Chan-Schura, Kluke von Klugenau, one of the bravest generals in the Caucasus, instantly setting out for Avaria, collected on his way the scattered troops of General Lasskoi, destroyed the aouls which refused to receive him, and made his entrance in triumph into Chunsach. There he set up as khan under the protection of Russia, Achmed-Mahomet-Mirza, and after having taken possession of the principal passes leading into Daghestan, returned without molestation to Temir-Chan-Schura.

Schamyl persevered, nevertheless, in his attempts to conquer the Avarians. In the year 1835, he captured the strong aoul of Gotsatl, and penetrated as far into the country as Chunsach, whence however he was obliged speedily to retire on the coming up of General Reout with a very much larger force. In the year following, his efforts were again thwarted by the determined resistance of Hadji-Murad, as well as by a want of unanimity among his own followers growing out of the continued rivalry between himself and Taschaw-Hadji.

But the year 1837 was destined to bring along in its course two important events which should settle forever the question of Schamyl's right to the imamship, and show the great superiority of his genius over that of all his rivals. The first of them was the complete overthrow he brought upon Count Iwelitsch, who had been sent to cut him off at the aoul Aschiltach; and the second was his heroic defence at Tiletli, a strongly fortified aoul in the district of Gumbet.

The latter achievement was especially memorable. Opposed to him was General

Fesi at the head of eight battalions of regular troops, and about twelve thousand militia drawn from that portion of Daghestan subject to Russia. These forces were also flushed with victory, for General Fesi after having marched from Derbend to Chunsach had erected a citadel there, had driven Ali Bey, one of Schamyl's murids, out of the fort of Akhulgo, and had then come to the rescue of lieutenant Butschkieff, who with a considerable detachment was hard pressed by Schamyl himself in the neighborhood of Tiletli.

After the union of these two forces the murids were but a handful in comparison. But their leader determined to make a stand, and to hold Tiletli, of which he had got possession, to the last. The Russians having the advantage not only of superior numbers but also of artillery, of which the Circassians were at that time entirely destitute, attempted immediately to carry the place by storm. In this they failed; but finally after very severe losses they succeeded in getting possession of one half of the aoul. Yet with such valor and intelligence was the other portion defended, that General Fesi was content to give over fighting, and fortify himself where he was. Schamyl did the same; and with a courage which excited the admiration of his followers, established his head-quarters in the face of the enemy, only a screen of a few houses intervening.

In this situation General Fesi could not remain long for want of provisions. But to retreat in the face of an enemy victorious because not subdued would be attended with disgrace if not with danger. Accordingly the Russian commander, disquieted besides by rumors of revolt in different parts of Daghestan, resolved to come to terms with his adversary, and retire under cover of them.

To accomplish this purpose, and yet do it in such a way as to give the color of a great triumph to what was in reality a most humiliating check, was a problem not after all of very difficult solution. All that was necessary was to require of Schamyl to take an oath of fealty to the emperor on the condition of being left in possession of not only Tiletli, but all the Lesghian highlands. And this Schamyl would be ready enough to do provided he might have the privilege of making the engagement in the presence of neither murids nor Russians. For an oath taken under such circumstances would be no oath at all, inasmuch as Schamyl holding to the Mahometan as well as Romanist doctrine that no faith is to be kept with infidels, and considering the Muscovites to be not only such but even half devils, and *feræ naturæ*, would feel himself in conscience under no obligations whatever to abide by what he had sworn to.

So it was arranged. Schamyl took the oath of fealty to the emperor in the presence of Achmed-Mahomet-Mirza, the new khan of Avaria, and gave hostages. By both parties the ceremony was regarded as a farce; but in virtue of it General Fesi retired from the enemy's country in safety, and sent his despatches to the commander-in-chief, summing up the results of the campaign of 1837, as follows: —

"A fortress built in Chunsach; all Avaria pacified; a number of previously unconquered mountain tribes subjected; many aouls and fortified places destroyed; Tiletli taken by storm; and Schamyl so hard pressed as to be obliged to swear fealty to the emperor forever and ever."

Accordingly in Tiflis and St. Petersburg it was for a time believed that Schamyl had submitted, and that the Lesghian highlands and all Daghestan were to be incorporated into the empire. At the same time the very clever General Fesi, covered with imperial praises, stars, and garters, was regarded by all as the hero of the war of the Caucasus.

XXXII.

ISSUES PROCLAMATIONS.

In consequence of these successes the fame of Schamyl went abroad through all the Lesghian country, as the greatest chieftain since the days of Khasi-Mollah. Taschaw-Hadji, unable any longer to set himself in opposition to the general will, publicly acknowledged the supremacy of his rival, and became thenceforth one of his most devoted supporters. Many tribes also who before had favored the Russians, or at least had not taken sides with the murids, now rallied around the new leader whose deeds were everywhere made the theme of declamation by the ulema and of song by the bards. "Schamyl is Imam and the second prophet of Allah," was the universal cry;

and multitudes came in from all sides but to see the face of one who by word of mouth, and without drawing a sword, had driven the army of invasion out of the highlands.

Taking advantage of this rising tide of favor, Schamyl issued various proclamations to his army and the tribes, one of which was as follows: —

"In the name of Allah, the almighty, the merciful!

"Praised be his name who hath led us in a path of light, and hath made us strong in his holy faith! Praised be he who hath laid the foundations of his power in the mountains, and hath set us to guard and to keep it; who hath strengthened our arm for the overthrow of the enemy, and hath made our tongue eloquent in declaring his doctrines unto all believers; who in the drops of rain sendeth us his blessing, whose love shines down upon us out of the stars, and whose mercy is infinite unto all who believe in his name!

"Ye warriors of Daghestan! When the leader of the Russians sent forth his call to you in the month of Schewal to seduce you from your faith in the truth of my mission, there arose doubt and murmuring among you; and many of you became unfaithful and forsook me. Then I was angry and said in my heart — The unsteadfast! they have verified the words of the Prophet when he saith,

"'God showeth you his wonders that ye may be wise; but your heart is harder than stone, yea, harder than stone; for among the rocks are the sources of the brooks; out of the rock when cloven asunder flow the waters; and smitten with the fear of the Almighty the great stones fall down from the tops of the mountains. But of a truth unto God are known all your doings!'

"But with the few, they who remained faithful, I went forth against the unbelievers, slew their leader, and drove them away in flight. When then ye saw that God was with me, ye returned repenting, and desired to be admitted once more into the ranks of the warriors, and I received you. I led you from victory to victory, and promised you God's forgiveness for your fault if ye continued in the faith as it is written in the book of the Prophet when he saith,

"'They who return and fight for their faith

in God, they shall be partakers of his mercy, for he is merciful and slow to anger.'

"Ye have seen how small was the number of our warriors in comparison with the hosts of the enemy, and yet they gave way to us, for strength is with the believers. The Russians have taken Akhulgo and have razed its walls. Allah permitted this to chastise you for your unbelief; for he knows all your projects and all your thoughts. But I mocked at the power of your enemies, and drove them from Aschiltach, and smote them at Tiletli, and turned their deeds to shame. When afterwards the Pacha (General Fesi) with his great army drew near Tiletli to revenge the slain, and when in spite of our brave resistance, he succeeded in taking possession of one half the aoul, so that day after day we looked for the last decisive struggle, then suddenly Allah lamed his arm and darkened his sight so that he could not use his advantages, but hastened away whence he came. No one drove our enemies save their evil consciences, for their unbelief made them afraid, and they fled to escape from the sight of the true believers.

"So doth God punish those who walk not in his ways! But unto us hath he said through his Prophet,

"'Whosoever wages the holy war for my sake, him will I lead in my ways.'

"Verily God is with those who do his will! Ye have seen that though great be the numbers of the unbelieving, they must ever fail. When they sent to Hamsad Bey, and summoned him to surrender, they said, 'Lay down your arms; all opposition is vain; the armies which we send against you are like as the sands on the sea-shore innumerable!' But I answered them in his name and said, 'Our hosts are like the waves of the sea which wash away the sands and devour them!'

"Ye have seen that my words came to pass. But the looks of the Russians are falsehood, and their words are lies. We must destroy the works of their hands, and slay them wherever we find them, in the house or in the field, by force or by cunning, so that their swarms shall vanish from the face of the earth. For they multiply like lice, and are as poisonous as the snakes that crawl in the steppe of Muhan. Ye have seen that the anger of God follows them. But unto us hath the Almighty said by his Prophet,

"'Whosoever goeth forth to fight for his faith and persevereth unto the end, him will God reward and bestow upon him his mercy.'

"And further hath God spoken unto us by his Prophet, saying,

"'Say not of those who fall striving for the faith, They are dead, but say rather, They live; for this understand ye not.'

"Therefore lay to heart that which I have declared unto you, and be strong, and hold fast together like the tops of the mountains above your heads, and forget not the words of the Prophet when he saith,

"'Slay the enemies of God; drive them out of the places whence they have driven you; for temptation is worse than death.' Amen."

XXXIII.

HIS HEAD-QUARTERS AT AKHULGO.

The Russians took a year to recover from the disastrous effects of General Fesi's feat of arms at Tiletli, attempting nothing in 1838, beyond several small and unsuccessful expeditions into the highlands, and contenting themselves with making preparations for the great campaign of the season following. On the other hand, so general was the enthusiasm among the tribes in favor of Schamyl and the war of independence, that he succeeded in collecting under his banners the greatest military force which had been seen in those regions since the days when Nadir-Shah overran Daghestan. The mountains were filled with his murids, who went from aoul to aoul preaching the new doctrine of the second prophet of Allah, and summoning all the warriors to rally around the chieftain commissioned by heaven to deliver the land from the threatened bondage to Russia. These missionaries in arms having friends and relatives in all the tribes, obtained everywhere a hearing and a foothold. The aouls which refused to join their party were threatened with destruction; and if they persisted in their refusal, their flocks and herds were driven off, their lands and vineyards laid waste, and their habitations razed to the ground. From others whose fidelity was to be suspected, hostages were taken. Schamyl would allow of no neutrality; whoever was not for him was against him. Accordingly by the end of the year 1838 he had rebuilt the forts which had been destroyed by the enemy the season previous, and had so far extended his rule that all of the Lesghian highlands lying north of Avaria, including Andi, Gumbet, Salatan, and Koissubui, together with a considerable portion of Tchetchenia, and all the more mountainous districts of Daghestan, were subject to him.

His head-quarters he established in the aoul

Akhulgo, a Tartar name signifying a gathering place in time of trouble, and now famous in Circassian annals for the siege sustained there in the campaign following. It is situated in the district of Koissubui, on the right bank of the Andian branch of the Koissu near its junction with the main stream, only a short distance northwest of Himri, and about sixty wersts by the most direct route from the Russian line. Like an eagle's nest it is perched on the top of an isolated, conical peak of rock, rising on one side perpendicularly six hundred feet above the Koissu, and of such fantastic formation as to lead to the saying that it was by divine permission the work of the devil. The river nearly surrounds it. On the top is the aoul, which is divided into old and new Akhulgo, being together a circumference of something less than a couple of wersts. A narrow path admitting only two persons to walk abreast, winds up the rock, which has three terraces formed by nature, and favorably situated for defence. Around in the near distance rise other less elevated rocks and cliffs, some of them tufted with oaks and beeches, others naked and time-stained, and all together forming a scene of such stern wildness as was well fitted for a hiding-place of liberty, or for its immolation.

The experience of the war having already proved that the high towers of stone such as had been built in the highlands up to the time of the death of Khasi-Mollah, were worse than useless as a means of defence against the Russian artillery, inasmuch as their defenders were exposed to be buried under their ruins, Schamyl instructed, it is said, by Polish deserters, now changed entirely the system of his fortifications. To prevent his defences at Akhulgo from being toppled down by the enemy's cannon, he made them to consist mainly of trenches, earthen parapets, and covered ways, while the saklis, which are a kind of hut built of loose stones, partly underground, were also converted into regular casements. These various fortifications, arranged with much skill, commanded all the approaches to the fortress, and everywhere exposed an attacking enemy to a great number of cross-fires. The rifle would indeed have to serve instead of cannon; but in the hands of the Circassian, though not discharged very rapidly inasmuch as it is cleaned after every shot, it was a weapon the Russians had good cause to dread.

Made strong therefore both by nature and by art, Akhulgo was the rock on which Schamyl resolved to plant his standard in the struggle for life and death known to be at hand. Herein he collected a large supply of provisions and munitions of war; hither he brought, as to a place of safety, many of the families of his murids; and here he kept in custody the hostages which had been taken from the tribes of Koissubui, Gumbet, and Andi. The garrison was composed of the flower of his warriors; while some fifteen thousand men besides, partly mounted and partly on foot, stood ready for the fight, every one having taken a solemn oath to drive back the Russians or perish in the attempt.

But while Akhulgo was the place where Schamyl had resolved to make a final stand for the liberty of the mountains, there were other points also where he proposed to stop, if possible, the march of the invaders. It was in the plan of the campaign which he had drawn up that when the Russians advanced from their forts in lower Daghestan they should be attacked in the rear by the Tchetchenians who had espoused his side in the contest, and whose position on the Koissu was favorable to the execution of such a manœuvre. But in case the enemy should succeed in penetrating into the mountains, the aoul of Buturnay was fixed upon as the point where the first resistance should be made; while a detachment of friendly Tcherkejians, or Salatanians, about three thousand strong, were to attack the enemy in the rear. In case, however, of a defeat at Buturnay, his troops would fall back upon a still stronger position at Arguani, and which during the year had been fortified in every way possible. After that, also, there would remain the natural barrier of the swiftly flowing Koissu; and finally Akhulgo itself, beyond which no further retreat was thought of, as there he and all his murids would either conquer or die.

It was a plan of campaign well devised, provided only the tribes appointed to attack the enemy in the flank and rear could be relied upon; but without their efficient coöperation the only chance of successful resistance would be on the rock of Akhulgo.

XXXIV.

THE SIEGE OF AKHULGO.

In the month of May, 1839, all things being ready, the Russian expedition commenced its march into the mountains. General Grabbe, an active and resolute officer in command of the left flank of the army of the Caucasus, had collected from the fortresses along the line where it crosses the Sulak, a force of nine battalions and seventeen pieces of artillery. They were his very best troops, including a part of the celebrated regiment "Count Paskievitsch," and with them he pressed forward with such rapidity towards Buturnay, and then attacked it with such impetuosity, that Schamyl was obliged at once to relinquish all hope of making a stand there. His allies, the Tcherkejians, taken by surprise at the suddenness of the enemy's advance, had not time to come to his assistance; the Salatanians were overawed by the extraordinary display of force made on their borders; and the Tchetchenians, alarmed by the bold face with which the Russian commander opened the campaign, and by his success at several minor points of conflict, took counsel of prudence, and failed to make the promised diversion on the line.

Schamyl, therefore, after a two hours' resistance fell back on Arguani. Here relying on a stronger position, and finding himself at the head of about ten thousand men, he awaited the coming up of the enemy. The contest which then took place lasted two days. Schamyl lost nearly fifteen hundred men in killed and wounded, and was beaten. It was the most bloody fight which had then occurred in the history of the war, and would have put an end at once to the campaign had not the Lesghians, every man of them, been determined to stand by their Imam and their liberty to the last. Instead, therefore, of scattering after a defeat so decisive, as might have been expected of mountaineers so little accustomed to regular warfare, they heroically threw themselves into Akhulgo.

The invaders having at length taken possession of both banks of the Koissu, and easily repulsed an attack of six thousand mountaineers led on by Achwerdu Mohamet, who had recently deserted from the Russian service, set themselves down on the twelfth of June before Akhulgo, closely investing it. General Grabbe hoped at first to induce the enemy to surrender by showering them with bombs, balls, and rockets; but while he succeeded in destroying many of the fortifications and stone houses, the subterranean defences remained undamaged. From these and the works on the terraces the besieged answered with their rifles, sparing indeed of their ammunition, but taking an unerring, deadly aim. Nowhere could the Russians show a head above their defences without imminent risk of losing it. Nor was their entire force scarcely adequate to man the posts; so that frequently the same troops who had worked all day in the trenches were obliged to stand guard during a portion of the night. Still they worked with hearty good-will, gradually carrying forward their batteries, cutting their way through the soft, porous rock, and sheltering themselves from the rifle-balls of the enemy by means of gabions and stone walls. During the early part of the siege the Russian camp was abundantly supplied with provisions; the Koissu gave them abundance of good water; the neighboring forests furnished wood for cooking the evening's soup; their fragrant boughs made easy beds at night; while numerous watch fires warmed the feet of the sleeping soldiers as they lay stretched beneath the stars. Even a certain degree of hilarity prevailed in the camp, so different from the prison of the krepost, where the daily drill, the appointed roll of the drum, and the enforced dance and song but poorly relieved the still, dull monotony. But the mirth was often ill-timed; for when refreshed by the evening's pottage and his cup of *wodka*, the Cossack sat carolling a ditty or meditating on the charms of the fair one left behind on the Don, suddenly a ball from the rifle of some watchful mountaineer would send him tumbling headlong into the Koissu. Or when the grey-coated grenadiers in the intervals between the roar of the artillery and the tumult of the trumpets, feeling their hearts stirred by a sudden enthusiasm, would break out into chanting, the half devotional, half martial air would often prove a dirge for some poor comrade struck down with the chorus on his lips by the ball of an invisible enemy.

The enthusiasm on the other side was less gay, but more intense. Besides the crack of the rifle, the only sounds from the fortress which fell down on the air when it was still, were the muezzin's call to prayer, or the shout of triumph when some frenzy-driven murid, sallying from his hiding-place, leaped suddenly into the midst of an exposed party of the enemy, and at the price of his own life sent twice, thrice, four times as many unbelieving souls to hell. For in the progress of the siege many a warrior who was doomed by his oath to death, and was become impatient of the hour, grasping a shaska in his right hand, a pistol in his left, and holding a poniard clenched between his teeth, sprang down from the rocks upon some too adventurous squad of the enemy — as terrible an apparition as a ghost, or a bomb-shell — discharging his pistol at the breast of one, cleaving with his shaska the head of another, and then rushing shaska in one hand and poniard in the other, upon the rest, until he fell pierced through with bayonets, but having first sweetened the bitterness of death with a terrible vengeance. Of such heroic self-sacrifice is the Circassian capable!

Twice was the moon renewed in the slow progress of this siege. At length, having previously got possession of one of the detached towers of the fortress, and having been reinforced by five battalions and nine pieces of artillery, the Russians, despairing of reducing the place by blockade, attacked it by storm. But they did not get above the first terrace; and from that they were beaten back with severe loss, — of the three battalions of the splendid regiment "Count Paskievitsch," which led the assault, only one returning. Nevertheless, General Grabbe was not to be disheartened. Another and still another assault was made; and after a loss of nearly two thousand men the second terrace was finally carried. Then Schamyl seeing that his fortunes were becoming desperate sent a request to the Russian commander to treat respecting terms of peace. What his intentions were in so doing is not known; though it was the opinion of General Grabbe that he was not sincere; and when the latter demanded Schamyl's son as a hostage previously to the opening of negotiations, the matter was dropped. Probably the Imam was desirous of making an arrangement similar to that which under somewhat similar circumstances had been agreed upon with General Fesi; but he had now a different man to deal with.

The contest therefore was recommenced on the seventeenth of August with new fury. Then for four successive days Akhulgo was a scene of heroism equalled only by its horror. The Russian soldiers evinced that ferocious bravery of which the serf nature is capable when its blood is up, while the Circassians, driven to despair, sought to avenge beforehand the lives they so gallantly laid down. High on the battlements, as at intervals the smoke of the two hostile fires cleared away, could be seen female forms, shaska or rifle in the little hand, encouraging the warriors by their side, pressing on with them wherever the danger was most imminent, and displaying a heroism greater even than that of their own amazons of old, inasmuch as they fought for their lords as well as for liberty.

But fortune finally favored the besiegers. Their sappers having carried a covered way up to the foot of a portion of the fortress which had newly been constructed, and the Circassians becoming anxious to learn the cause of the strange noises constantly heard beneath their feet, a party of the latter imprudently went out to reconnoitre, when the chief of a battalion who lay in wait with his men on the second terrace, seizing upon the advantage offered, not only drove the exploring party back into the fortress, but also went in with them. The Circassians within, however, seeing that the Russians were mixed up with their own comrades refrained from firing. This gave the other battalions time to hasten to the support of the party which they saw had gained the summit, when a hand to hand conflict ensued in which both sides fought, the one with the bravery of despair, the other with that of victory. But superior numbers prevailed; and four times stormed the fortress fell. Of the mountaineers that lay dead on the top of the rock the Russians counted, according to some of their accounts, fifteen hundred, according to others, more likely to be true, seven hundred; of the wounded, from nine hundred to five hundred; while their own loss was set down as considerably less than one half these numbers. Several hundred prisoners also were taken, consisting of women and children; for of men there were none left. With the blood of these the Koissu was already red, and their bodies were thrown in afterwards.

But Schamyl, who had often been seen during the final conflict surrounded by his white turbaned murids, was nowhere to be found. The fortress, all the approaches to which were strictly guarded, was ransacked; every nook and corner explored; but the Imam was nowhere to be found. Alas! for General Grabbe, that but one man should escape from Akhulgo, and he Schamyl. His single head would have made up for the loss of the three thousand Russian heads laid low in the siege; but without it the victory was barren, all its spoils a mere rock in the mountains!

The manner of Schamyl's escape was kept secret by him, as before had been the case at Himri and at Chunsach; but among the reports respecting it which were circulated in the mountains, the following one was most generally credited.

On the fall of the fortress a number of its defenders took refuge in certain caves and holes in the rock, into which they let themselves down by means of ladders. In one of these was Schamyl with a few of his murids. Attacked by the enemy, this one held out longer than the others; but the rock being guarded on all sides, escape was thought impossible. The murids, however, having devised a plan for preserving the life of their chief by the loss of their own, constructed from materials previously collected in the cave, a raft of sufficient size to carry several persons, and letting it down at night into the river below, then followed themselves. The guard on the bank observing this manœuvre, immediately gave chase to the raft, those on horseback plunging into the stream, those on foot running along the bank, and all together pouring their fire into the little party of murids among whom was, as they supposed, Schamyl. But the attention of the enemy once turned away from the cave, the wily chieftain let himself down into the water, swam the river, and in another moment was safe under the protection of the rocks and the forest.

Certain it is that early in the month of September, Schamyl reappeared in the aoul Siassan, in the woods of Itchkeria. There, partly for the sake of ransoming the families of his nearest relatives and most devoted murids taken captive in Akhulgo, he sued for peace, and offered to give in pledge of sincerity two of his own sons as hostages. But General Grabbe insisting as a preliminary condition that Schamyl should take up his residence in an aoul friendly to the Russians, the negotiations were not proceeded with.

Thereupon, General Grabbe having razed Akhulgo, having laid a contribution in sheep and cattle on some districts, taken hostages from others, and received the bread and salt of submission from all the aouls through which he passed, returned in triumph to Temir-Chan-Schura. Great thereupon was the rejoicing in all the fortresses of the Russian line — in all the Cis and Trans-Caucasian provinces — and in St. Petersburg itself, where the emperor ordered a medal to be struck commemorative of this brilliant feat at arms, and copies of it to be distributed among the brave soldiers who had taken part in it.

XXXV.

THE EXPEDITION AGAINST DARGO.

THE defeat at Akhulgo did not turn away from Schamyl the hearts of his countrymen. On the contrary, now thrice delivered by Allah out of the hands of the infidels, he was regarded by them with the greater veneration. Though escaped with only his life and his arms, when he appeared in the aouls of Itchkeria, a territory lying north of the Andian branch of the Koissu, the mountaineers received him as a prophet come directly from God, and mounting their horses followed him. The news of his coming ran before him through all the highlands; the warriors half drew their shaskas at hearing it; the chieftains of the Tchetchenians who had received the cross of St. George from the Russians, tore it from their breasts; and the bards striking with a frenzy of inspiration their lyres, chanted the miraculous deliverance and great deeds of this successor of Mahomet.

Thus going from aoul to aoul preaching faith in Allah and war against his enemies, sending out also disciples to visit in his name the remoter districts, threatening death to all who held with the Russians, here driving away flocks and herds, and there taking hostages, he in a few months succeeded in rallying around his standards great numbers of the Tchetchenians, of the Lesghians, and of the various tribes of Daghestan. Disgusted by the treatment he received at the hands of the Russians, as was also the case with most of the highland tribes who had recently been obliged to submit their necks to the yoke of bondage, even his old enemy Hadji-Murad came over to the side of the Imam, bringing the greater part of Avaria with him. The spirit of fanatic war swept over the whole eastern Caucasus like a tempest; and those tribes, like the Salatanians, who from the nearness of their position to the Russian line were obliged nominally to acknowledge the supremacy of the czar, burned in their hearts to join again the standard of revolt.

His head-quarters Schamyl now established in Dargo, an aoul consisting of about seventy houses, and situated some fifty miles northwest from Akhulgo, in that part of Tchetchenia inhabited by the Itchkerians. Though an open aoul, Dargo was sufficiently protected by the mountains and the thick forests which everywhere covered them; for here the primeval woods had never been disturbed by the axe of any pioneers of civilization. The oaks stretched out against the sky their twisted branches crowned with the glory of two centuries; the beeches with their innumerable leaves spread out a wider shade than those which in Italy inspired the pastoral reed of Virgil; the round-topped elms towered high above the gracefully pointed birches, and the trembling poplars; while below in many localities a vast variety of flower-bearing plants, vines, and creepers formed a tangled web as beautiful to the eye and fragrant to the sense as to the feet impenetrable.

But instructed by the disasters of the campaign of Akhulgo, Schamyl resolved no more to concentrate his forces and attempt to meet the enemy face to face. Accordingly, apportioning them among his chief murids, such as Achwerdu-Mahomet, Schwaib-Mollah, Ulubuy-Mollah, Taschaw-Hadji, Dschewad-Khan, and Hadji-Murad, besides retaining a considerable force under his own command, he was enabled to overawe a very great number of tribes, and to threaten the Russians simultaneously at various points. Inroads were made at one time into the land of the Kumucks, that of Schamchal, and Avaria; at another, the Russian line was threatened; and again, the forts were attacked on the road to Kisliar. If hard pushed the murids retreated; wherever opportunity offered they struck a blow and suddenly retired; those tribes who wavered in their allegiance found themselves unexpectedly visited with retribution; and when the Tchetchenians, aggrieved by Schamyl's apparent neglect of their interests, took advantage of a wound received by him to send messengers to Tiflis to sue for peace, immediately he appeared in their midst, terrifying rather than winning them back to the cause of the patriots.

Such remained the state of affairs until the year 1842, when General Grabbe, less benefited by experience than his antagonist, resolved to make an expedition against Dargo, similar to that of Akhulgo. Differing in his views of the proper mode of conducting the war from his superior, Governor-general Golowin, who resided in Tiflis, away from the scene of actual hostilities, and who was in favor of the less aggressive system of a blockade, he had then just returned from St. Petersburg, whither he had gone to explain his plans of action to the imperial cabinet, and whence partly in consequence of his representations the emperor had sent his minister of war, Prince Tschernitscheff, to inspect the military posts in both Cis and Trans-Caucasia. To surprise then the Prince, upon his arrival on the left flank of the line of operations, by a splendid feat of arms which should serve to demonstrate the correctness of his own theory of procedure, General Grabbe undertook the expedition against Dargo.

On the twenty ninth of May, accordingly, he set out at the head of thirteen battalions, or about eight thousand six hundred foot-soldiers. Of cavalry, on account of the difficult nature of the march, he took none, excepting a few Cossacks to attend upon his own person. Every soldier was loaded down with sixty cartridges, and provisions for eight days in his knapsack. The guns, four and six pounders, were drawn each by four horses; and there were besides a few baggage-wagons, which were dragged with still more difficulty over ground where wheels never rolled before.

At the close of the first day's march, the soldiers as they lay around their camp-fires congratulated themselves that they had not heard on the way the report of a single rifle; though some of the sharpshooters of the vanguard pretended that they had seen here and there the slender form of a Circassian flitting like an apparition or a wood-demon behind the large-stemmed trees. But after the soldiers, having cooked and eaten their pottage and swallowed the refreshing draught of *wodka*, had stretched their limbs wearied with the hard day's march upon the sweet-smelling herbs and branches, suddenly a rattling volley of musketry brought every man to his feet. The Circassians were upon them. But in the dark they could not discern the enemy scattered about among the trees, and could fire only wherever they saw a flash. The contest, however, did not prove to be a serious one, from lack of certain aim, comparatively few falling on either side; but the firing continued at intervals through the night effectually scared away sleep, and thereby rendered the soldiers less fit for the duties of the day following.

When the morning dawning lit up the darkness of the woods, not a Circassian was to be seen. The enemy had in fact begun to put his new tactics into execution, worrying the march he had no wish to arrest, and giving the column of invaders only a foretaste of the retribution which awaited them for daring to profane by their presence the woods free from the foundations of the world. During the freshness of the early morning the column advanced unhindered save by the unevenness of the ground, the thick-standing trees, and the undergrowth which in many places almost barred the way which it beautified. But towards noon, as the route led through a ravine in the forest, the firing recommenced. A considerable body of Circassians posted behind the trees poured a murderous volley in upon the vanguard. The number of the wounded increased to such a degree that the horses and wagons were not sufficient for their transportation. Thereupon several of the higher officers, their minds weighed down with sad presentiments, advised the commanding general to relinquish an expedition which at every step seemed to be involved in greater difficulties and more serious dangers. But the heart of General Grabbe was set upon entertaining the imperial minister of war with the celebration of a great victory; and he kept on.

On the second evening of the march the tents were pitched in a small, open meadow in the hills, skirted by the forest; yet the weary soldiers were not lulled to sleep by the soft murmuring of the night wind in the tree tops, nor by the silvery tinkling of the brook which flowed through the green; but all night long the sharp crack of rifles and the whizzing of bullets drove away repose, and filled the before silent woods with the tumult and the pains of a pandemonium. Nor did the rising sun scatter the enemy with the darkness, but at every step of the morning's march the pitiless missiles of destruction were hurled from invisible foes upon the now nearly decimated column.

Twelve wersts more, and it would be at the end of its march. The little aoul of Dargo, perched on a hill-top, was even descried in the transparent distance. But the eyes which were turned towards it beheld death staring them in the face still nearer; and at length General Grabbe, seeing that to reach his destination however near would imperil the entire column, — and that for a purpose which by this time he must have perceived to be utterly futile, — gave the order to retreat.

Then as the Circassians, estimated to have been nearly six thousand strong, saw that the advanced guard had wheeled about, and that the column was retracing its footsteps, their enthusiasm mounted to frenzy; and slinging their rifles behind their backs they rushed upon the enemy's centre shaska in hand. Several times they broke through it. But the well-disciplined soldiers restoring as often the disordered ranks fought bravely; for they fought for their lives, the Circassians giving no quarter. Still, as the day wore away many a comrade wearied out by both marching and fighting, exhausted from loss of blood, and tormented by thirst still more than by his wounds, dropped behind the column, and throwing away his knapsack in despair, resigned himself to death at the hands of the first warrior who should come up with him.

At night no soul was allowed any other sleep than that of death. Though the enemy was reluctant to waste his powder in the darkness, yet he kept close by the side of his victims; while the wolves of the forest followed howling behind. As the captain at sea when the tempest roars around his vessel ready to ingulf it stands watching through the dismal hours of the night by the wheel, so did the officers of this forlorn column stand around the bivouac fires vociferating orders which in the confusion and the darkness could but imperfectly be executed. And when at last day broke over the mountain tops, the first beautiful day of June, the soldiers looked at its blush in the east with faces pallid with watching and haggard with despair.

Three hundred times, as was estimated, did

the soldier discharge his musket, until from want of cleaning it could be used no longer. The officers, who to prevent their coats from being a mark for the rifles had put on those of common soldiers, still recognized by their sharp-eyed foe by means of the superior cast of lineaments and the manlier carriage, were picked off — thirty-six out of sixty. A drummer taken captive was compelled to beat his drum as a signal indicating the direction of the march, but which led those who followed its call into the midst of their enemies. Six cannon at one time fell into the hands of the Circassians, who in attacking the artillery especially displayed a strength of muscle in wielding the shaska, and an agility of limb in parrying or avoiding the bayonet-thrust, which excited the wonder as well as the dread of the enemy.

But the brave Lieutenant-colonel Wittert, burning with shame at the loss of the guns, led on his men to the rescue; when took place one of the most terrible encounters on the march. The officers led the attack sword in hand and the hurra in their throats; while the soldiers advanced on the run with fixed bayonets. The first man, Lieutenant-colonel Hahn, who laid his hand on a cannon, fell back dead; and many shared his fate; for the mountaineers fought for the possession of "the emperor's pistols" like tigers for their prey; some climbing into the tops of the trees the better to take aim at the rescuers below; and when hit themselves frequently lodging in the branches, where they continued to hang a convenient carrion for the foul birds of the forest.

Schamyl arriving at the head of his riders, — alas! for him, too late, — attacked the column of invasion as it was about coming out of the forests. Having intrusted his foot-soldiers to his principal murids, he had been going the rounds of the aouls, collecting his mounted men, and not expecting that the enemy would so soon turn back. Had he arrived on their line of march two days earlier, not a Russian of them all would have ever again seen a krepost. As it was, two thousand left their bones in the woods to be picked by wolves and vultures. The rest succeeded in reaching Girsel-aoul, a fortress on the line about fifty miles north of Dargo, but in sorry plight indeed. Preparations had been made there for a military triumph, with salvos of cannon, music, and colors flying; and the minister of war, Prince Tschernitscheff, had most inopportunely arrived to witness it; but instead he beheld the battalions marching in with faintly beating drums, the men haggard from fatigue and want of food, their uniform tattered and blood-stained, and the officers sadder still at the loss of so many brave soldiers sacrificed in vain.

When some months afterward the minister of war made to the emperor his report on the state of affairs in the Caucasus, General Grabbe was immediately recalled, and his chief, Governor-general Golowin, likewise.

XXXVI.

HIS DOMESTIC LIFE.

Schamyl's head-quarters continued for several years to be at Dargo, where aided by Polish deserters he built a residence somewhat superior in style to the houses generally seen in the eastern Caucasus. It was surrounded by a double row of strong palisades with a filling of small stones and earth, and was approached through a single gateway guarded by sentinels. Near this, on the inner side, stood a tower for defence, irregular in shape, and built of stone. Still beyond was the principal building in the inclosure inhabited by the Imam and his harem. Like the tower, this was constructed of stones not, as is usually the case, smeared on the sides by clay, but laid in a kind of mortar; was of two stories, with a stairway outside leading to the chambers; had a verandah on one side and a balcony on the other; and was covered by a flat roof from which frowned a couple of Russian six-pounders. There were also several smaller outbuildings for the servants, the guard, and for the storing of provisions. Of these there were always kept on hand a considerable quantity, such as maize, wheat, barley, and millet, all preserved in large casks hollowed out of logs. In the inclosure was likewise a fountain of water brought down from the hills, besides stalls for horses, pens for cattle, and coops for poultry. A number of murids were always on guard about the establishment; and when Schamyl went to the mosque they walked by his side with drawn shaskas.

If built in other respects like the Circassian dwellings, as is probable, the house would have but a single door, only a few small windows to admit the light, and these very likely of either parchment or paper. Generally the floor is of hard earth, which is kept cleanly swept, is sprinkled in hot weather with water, and is partially covered with mats. Around two or three sides of the room runs the divan; the chimney is constructed in an outer wall not projecting into the room as in the houses of the western Caucasus; and there is very little furniture. The divan, however, answers the purpose of both seat and bed; for while during the daytime the inhabitants sit upon it on their heels after the fashion of the Turks, at night with the addition of mattresses, pillows, and coverlets, it is a sufficiently convenient couch for the Asiatic, who lies down to rest without undressing. In summer many persons have their mattresses spread under the verandah; or, wrapping themselves in their felt bourkas, lie down to their repose under the trees. But in winter all sleep around the fire, the warmest corner being always occupied by the master of the house, an elder, or a guest, in case there be one.

If the proprietor is rich the divan will be furnished at considerable expense, it being the custom of eastern Asia to lavish expenditure more upon the furniture of the habitation than upon the habitation itself. Covered with red leather and stuffed with hair, the divan is supplied with cushions of some dark, rich silk, and bolsters sprigged with gold and silver; its mattresses are bordered with velvet; the coverlet is of quilted brocade, or a gay muslin of various colors studiously arranged, and fringed with satin; and there may even be clean white sheeting. Above the divan the walls will be hung with beautifully wrought matting or carpets brought from Stamboul. Small tablets likewise are sometimes placed around the room, inscribed with verses from the Koran in the Arabic characters. But the principal ornament of the walls are the arms, which, suspended from wooden pegs, gleam and flash in the fire-light — sabres, pistols, rifles, coats of mail, bows and quivers, besides bridles, saddles, and housings. For on entering the house, the warrior lays aside all his weapons save the poniard, and his guest does the same.

The apartments for females and children are always separate from the others, and are frequently in a building by itself. Here with no look-out from windows on the passing world, the news of which it would be an impropriety in a Circassian to question his wives about, they ply their tasks, spinning, weaving, embroidering, and knitting silver lace in an obscurity illumined by scanty rays of sunlight. The walls of these apartments are hung with dresses, not with arms. Strung also upon lines across the room are various specimens of female industry, as embroidered napkins, handkerchiefs, veils, silken bodices, and anteris glittering with threads of gold and silver; in the corners are piles of large boxes containing the bedding of the house; while on shelves are arranged china and glass ware, with various culinary utensils of brass, copper, or glazed pottery, kept for show, while the wooden are for use. Here also the loom has its place, at which are woven all the plainer stuffs worn in the family.

It falls to woman's lot in these mountains as well as out of them to prepare the food of the household. The Circassian still retaining much of the patriarchal simplicity of living, eats when he is hungry, without regard to set hours; nor is there any gathering of the family around the social board, every member generally taking his meals by himself, and the males under no circumstances eating with the females. The flesh of sheep and goats is the kind of meat in most common use. This is prepared in savory ragouts well seasoned with salt, pepper, coriander seeds, and capsicums; or, being cut in pieces, is roasted on small iron spits, the morsels taken from the saddle, and the fat of sheep-tails being considsidered the most dainty. Meats also are preserved by salting, smoking, and drying. Still oftener, however, they are boiled, and their juices eaten in a kind of pottage with millet in it, being the same as the Sclavonian and Polish *cachat*, the use of which extends as far west as the Adriatic, while on the southern side of the Caucasus, even to Central Asia, the pilaff is made with rice. Throughout the Caucasus millet is the favorite grain, of which cakes are made by being baked on hot flat stones or iron plates. The wheaten loaf likewise is common in many localities, and so the cake of Turkey corn. All these different kinds of bread are eaten with honey, great quantities of which are taken from the hives of wicker-work or bark of trees, and of an exceedingly delicious quality, owing to the wild thyme and other aromatic herbs fed on by the bees. The Circassians have a good many vegetables, though they are not particularly fond of this kind of diet. Cucumbers which are apparently indigenous in these regions are, however, in much favor; and more or less use is made of melons, gourds, pumpkins, beets, onions, carrots, cabbages, asparagus, artichokes, and beans. Fish are still less liked, though the rivers abound in salmon-trout, and numerous other varieties. On the other hand, the consumption of fruit is very considerable, particularly of apples, pears, cherries, peaches, grapes, olives, figs, pomegranates, almonds, walnuts, and chestnuts, many of which kinds grow wild in the woods.

All Circassians are very fond of a kind of sour milk peculiar to the East, called by them *skhou*, and by the Turks and Tartars *yaourte*. This is taken sometimes pure, sometimes flavored with a little sugar and rose-water, or is boiled with millet or maize. Said to be remarkably refreshing, its origin is traced back to Abraham, who obtained it directly from the Almighty; or as another tradition says, it was bestowed originally by an angel on Hagar when driven out from the house of her lord she was fainting with heat and thirst in the desert. It takes the place very much of spirituous and fermented liquors, in the use of which the mountaineers are exceedingly temperate. A kind of mead, not very potent, however, is made by them of millet, honey, and water, and is decidedly a superior beverage to

> The one called *kuas*, whereby the Russie lives,
> Small ware, water-like, but somewhat tart in taste.

This mead is the liquor principally drunk at feasts, and of this formerly were oblations poured out to the gods. More or less wine also is drunk in the Caucasus, always of a light quality, and more resembling champagne than the other wines of Europe. Its use being prohibited by the Koran, is discountenanced by the Sufis and Schamyl's party. Nevertheless there are here and there those among the faithful who continue to say,

> Ma sopra tutto nel buon vin ho fede ;
> E credo che sia salvo che gli crede.

And since latterly the Russians have introduced their brandy, the number of believers is not small, who, on mounting their steeds, will take a stirrup cup of schnapps when offered.

On the whole, the Circassians are remarkably temperate in both meats and drinks; in this simplicity of living, as in so many other respects, still preserving a striking resemblance to the manners and customs of the Greeks of the earliest ages. At their feasts and entertainments given to strangers, however, there is always a great profusion of dishes, which are served in succession on small, three-legged trays; and a generous host is known as a man of "forty tables." On journeys and warlike expeditions, on the contrary, the mountaineer is contented with barely, a little millet, sour milk, and honey, all of which are easily transported in leathern bottles at his saddle-bow. Nor at home on all ordinary occasions does he want more, a morsel of meat perhaps being added. But though simple the fare, its cookery is pronounced not bad even by Europeans; and the traveller has much less reason here than in some other oriental countries to demand of his host the *dish parasi*, or indemnification for the wear of his teeth.

For temperance of living Schamyl has always been remarkable even among his countrymen. His house accordingly has not been one of feasting, though a moderate number of guests are constantly entertained by him. Nor is it to be supposed that either of his three legitimate wives serve tables, however probable it may be that this office is performed by the handmaidens of whom, according to the fashion of the East, he keeps a certain number in his house, captured Russian females being especially preferred.

Of his wives one is an Armenian, and if the half that is told of her in the mountains be true, of a beauty not unlike that attributed by the noble English bard to Theresa.

> She had the Asiatic eye,
> Such as our Turkish neighborhood
> Hath mingled with the Polish blood,
> Dark as above us is the sky;
> But through it stole a tender light,
> Like the first moonrise of midnight;
> Large, dark, and swimming in the stream,
> Which seemed to melt to its own beam;
> *All* love, half languor, and half fire,
> Like saints that at the stake expire.

In severe dignity of features and stateliness of carriage the Armenian females are not unlike the Circassian and the Georgian. In these mountains, however, the former do not wear the brown mantle in which they wrap themselves at Constantinople, but long black veils which fall in graceful folds to the feet, and display the shape like the drapery of the old Greek statues. Beneath is a silken wrapper confined by a girdle richly ornamented with gold and silver. The trousers are full, and commonly of bright colored Indian cotton. Their headdress is generally a shawl gracefully twisted into the form of the turban; while their hands, fingers, and ears are always decorated with ornaments of gold and silver. In this attractive costume these fair ones from the south side of the mountains are highly esteemed by the Circassian chieftains, though few can afford to pay the high prices often demanded by their sires. For the Armenian merchant is the Jew of the Caucasus, and having sold every thing else, will even sell his country's daughters. Destitute of all patriotic feeling, his whole soul bound up in his gains, he brings into these mountains all the spirit of trade there is in them, ever calculating, figuring, discounting, and bargaining with a patience which ends only with life itself. So different is the spirit of man among the woods and snows of the Caucasus, and in the sunny vales which lie around the foot of Ararat.

Captives, male as well as female, are common in the households of the Circassian chiefs, and formed doubtless a part of Schamyl's domestic establishment. Generally they are put to hard labor in the fields; but the reports of barbarous treatment brought back by the few Russians who have escaped from slavery in the Caucasus are for the most part greatly exaggerated. Often, on the contrary, they become favorites with their masters, to whom they are serviceable in introducing European improvements. They invariably receive kind treatment at the hands of the females, and are frequently allowed to take wives and have households of their own. Still, as the Circassian carried away into captivity always regrets his native mountains and will return to them, if possible, so the lowlander often pines for the plains from which he has been torn. Treated ever so kindly the Cossack will sigh when he remembers the freedom with which he once roved the steppes, lance in hand, on his shaggy little steed; and the Kalmuck also when he thinks of his hut half buried in the sands on the shore of the Caspian, whence he was wont to sally forth with his falcon on his fist, and letting it fly at the heron, followed himself almost as swiftly on the gallop.

XXXVII.

PRINCE WORONZOFF AT DARGO.

Governor-general Golowin was succeeded by General Neidhart, an officer who had served with distinction in the war against Napoleon, and afterward in the bloody strife in Poland, and who had won the reputation of being not only an able commander, but a skilful administrator, and a man of sterling worth of character. He was sent into the Caucasus to carry out the system of defence and gradual conquest which had been approved of at St. Petersburg in opposition to that of aggressive invasion, the results of which had been so disastrous under his predecessor.

But it was by no mere change of men or

plans that such a master-spirit as Schamyl was to be conquered. Nothing daunted by the arrival on the scene of action of a new opponent, he broke through the Russian line, captured the fortress of Unzala, and devastated Avaria. While making Dargo his headquarters where he had collected considerable stores of ammunition and provisions, he with unabating zeal went the rounds of all the neighboring tribes, keeping alive the ardor of those who were friendly to him, and visiting with condign punishment those who took sides with the enemy. Neidhart standing mainly on the defensive was unable to make any progress in either conciliating or subjugating the highlanders, and at the end of two years had rather lost ground than gained it. He therefore in his turn was recalled in disgrace to give place to a commander the most distinguished who had been sent to the Caucasus since Jermoloff.

This was Prince, then Count Woronzoff. Having served like General Neidhart in the French and Polish wars, he had afterward, as governor of the Crimea, acquired such a degree of popularity as had not been enjoyed before since the days of Potemkin, the favorite of Catherine. The owner of forty thousand serfs, and said to be the handsomest Russian living after Nicholas himself, he possessed also the highest order of administrative talent, a complete knowledge of the art of war, and the most heroic qualities of character. Fully appreciating his worth the emperor in calling him to the command of the army of the Caucasus, invested him with such extraordinary powers as procured for him among the Circassians the title of "the Russian half-king." The power of life and death over the natives was given him; he was authorized to put officers in the army of every grade on trial for offences; could remove and appoint all civil functionaries up to the sixth grade; and could bestow various military honors and rewards without the confirmation of the emperor. This was indeed a generous gift of power, — and that simply for the sake of putting down the chieftain of a few rude tribes in the mountains.

But after having made it, the emperor became desirous once more of striking a blow such as should justify this change of administration, avenge the disaster of the expedition against Dargo, and even put an immediate end to the war. Nothing short of the capture of this same Dargo would answer his purposes. Such an undertaking was indeed contrary to the best judgment and wishes of the new commander; but expressly to gratify his sovereign, as he said, Woronzoff finally consented to lead another Russian column into the forests of Itchkeria.

It was in the summer of 1845, and only a few months after Woronzoff's arrival in the mountains. With a force of ten thousand infantry and a few hundred Cossacks, he set out for Dargo, taking instead of the northern track previously followed by General Grabbe, the route by the river Koissu and through the district of Andi. On their march to its principal aoul, called also Andi, the Russians were not attacked by the mountaineers, though closely watched by them. Here and there small parties would appear in the distance, but they seemed to be disposed, as usual, to spare their powder, and contented themselves with occasionally rolling down stones upon the heads of their adversaries as they passed through the narrower defiles. The column therefore advanced with good spirits, having full rations, confiding in their new leader, and rather underrating than dreading an enemy who attacked them with stones instead of bullets.

At Gogatel, a small fort situated south of the Andian range, which runs parallel with the Andian branch of the Koissu, Woronzoff established a depot of such provisions and munitions of war as could not conveniently be transported further. This was but a single day's journey from Dargo; and on the seventeeth of July, all preparations having been fully made, and summer being in mid-reign, the order of march was given out for the morrow.

The soldiers, lightly laden, set off cheerfully by the light of the resplendent dawn; and before the freshness of the morning was gone they had crossed by the pass of Retschel into the beech-woods of Itchkeria. Then began the fight. The hostile tribes of all the region round were up in arms, and waiting in the depths of the woods for the enemy. As his vanguard reached the first narrow and precipitous defile they were received by a murderous fire from behind numerous trunks of trees which, felled across the way, served as breastworks for the one party and obstacles to the progress of the other. Besides these barricades, the barriers no less difficult of removal, which were woven by nature, of thousands of vines and flower-bearing creepers, the narrowness and steepness of the paths, added to the opposition of the enemy, rendered the march so difficult that on an average it did not exceed one and a half wersts the hour. Still Woronzoff fought his way through; and as the shades of night began to gather under the woods he was in sight of Dargo. But it was the aoul in flames which, joined to the reappearing stars, now lit up the way; for Schamyl, having gathered together whatever of wood, straw, and grain could not be taken away, had set it all on fire, thereby leaving to the enemy the conquest of merely the blackened stone walls of the houses. Indeed the burning ruins of his own residence supplied the bivouac fires by which the weary soldiers cooked their evening meal, and then lay down to sleep.

The next day the fight was renewed.

Schamyl had retired with a force of about six thousand warriors to a height which commanded the aoul, and thence opened a fire upon the Russians with their own cannon, the trophies of former victories. The "emperor's pistols" consumed indeed too much powder to be fired with any great rapidity, nor did the mountaineers know how to take aim over a six-pounder as well as they did along the barrels of their rifles; still one ball came bounding into the very tent of the staff of officers, and it became necessary, therefore, in order to prevent accidents, to scale the height. After not a little hard fighting this was finally done at the point of the bayonet; but the Circassians retired, dividing the honors of the field with the enemy, for they carried off the guns.

Dargo was taken, but not Schamyl. What then was to be done? Woronzoff finally decided that he would send the half of his force back to Gogatel to get a supply of provisions, and on their return push through the woods and regain the Russian line by the route northward. But this movement on Gogatel gave the mountaineers another chance at their enemies. With Schamyl at their head and strengthened by reinforcements, they attacked the escort party both going and returning. The Circassians give themselves no rest until they have had blood for blood; and the two preceding days their own had flowed pretty freely. Not satisfied with the slow though certain work of the rifle they now rushed in upon the battalions, and with shaska and poniard fought hand to hand. Generals Wiktoroff and Passek fell defending themselves with their swords. Rain and tempest made the battle still more terrific. The brave General Klucke did his best; but when he arrived at Dargo he had left thirteen hundred of his men, together with the two generals, behind in the woods. Three hundred mules also with their packs, and a considerable number of wagons loaded with grain, besides one cannon, fell into the hands of the enemy.

But with what of the convoy was saved Count Woronzoff set out from Dargo on his return. The soldiers were put on half rations, and the horses had nothing to eat but grass. Through the valley of the Aksai, to the Russians a valley of death, inasmuch as General

Grabbe had before strewn it with his slain, led the way. Nor was it now scarcely less wet with blood. For Schamyl's men fought the retiring battalions step by step. Wherever the mountains projecting up to the very bank of the Aksai left only a narrow passage for the troops, the way was stopped by barricades. The Circassians taking aim from behind the rocks and the beech trees, brought down so many victims that the few horses of the Cossacks sufficed not to transport the wounded, so that whoever was disabled was necessarily abandoned to his fate.

When then the commander saw that so many of his brave soldiers were left behind to fall into the hands of a foe whose hate left no room in his breast for mercy, he resolved to make a halt, and send for reinforcements. Fortunately for him some natives who, bribed by large sums of gold, had undertaken under cover of night to carry despatches to the fortress of Girsel-aoul, succeeded in getting through, and conveying to the garrison intelligence of the hazardous situation of their countrymen. Thereupon three thousand infantry and three hundred Cossacks under General Freitag hastened to their relief. And great indeed was the joy of the famished battalions when their comrades arriving shared with them the contents of their knapsacks, took the wounded upon their horses, and helped to beat off the enemy. The march then proceeded without further difficulty, and on the first of August the conquerors of Dargo, less three thousand of their dead, arrived in safety at Girsel-aoul.

For this sad service of his master, heralded at St. Petersburg and through Europe as a great victory — and such are Russian victories in the Caucasus — Count Woronzoff was made a Prince! But when a few months afterward he met the emperor at Sebastopol for the purpose of exchanging views respecting the future conduct of the war, it is understood that the latter became at last fully convinced that the Caucasus could not be subjected by the method of direct invasion, but only by adhering to the policy of gradually drawing closer and closer around the mountains the line of the fortresses, in connection with the use of light, movable columns as a means of supporting them. Accordingly no more hostile expeditions into the interior have since been undertaken, and no more such triumphs as that at Dargo have been gazetted. Woronzoff, convinced himself that the successful termination of the war was to be hoped for only from long-continued perseverance in maintaining the armed blockade and active siege of the mountains, contented himself during the half a dozen years of his command in the Caucasus with attempting to carry these views into execution, and also in endeavoring to accomplish the Augean task of cleansing the administration of both government and army of the corrupt practices which had long prevailed in both. In the latter undertaking he met with a good degree of success; but in the former, though aided by an army in both Cis and Trans-Caucasia of from one hundred and fifty to two hundred thousand men, he made on the whole no progress. Nor have his successors, Generals Read and Mouravieff, been able to do more. The genius of Schamyl and the Circassian love of liberty, combined with the natural resistance of Caucasian rocks and forests, have proved to be more than a match for them.

XXXVIII.

SCHAMYL'S PROCLAMATION TO THE KABARDIANS.

Not only did the double wall of rocks and human breasts throbbing with the love of independence prove impenetrable to the Russian columns led on by a chief of transcendent abilities, but that wall was gradually strengthened and enlarged. Schamyl could not be kept within bounds. The year after the fall of Dargo he broke through the cordon of fortresses, and pouncing upon the neutral provinces of Kabarda, performed the most brilliant exploit in his whole career.

The Kabardas, the great and the little, are twin provinces lying on the northern side of the Caucasian range midway between the two seas, and in a north-westerly direction from the Lesghian and Tchetchenian highlands. It is a land of green valleys and sunny hill-sides, more broken on the side where it joins on to the mountains; softly undulating in the central portions; and to the north, where it falls down to the banks of the Terek and to the level of the steppes, a plain almost as smooth as a sheet of water. Here, until the coming of the Russians, a people mainly pastoral had kept their flocks and herds for centuries. Simple in their modes of life, yet trained to arms, they were of the blood of the gallant race of the Adighés or Circassians of the western Caucasus. Scarcely less lovers of freedom than the tribes who dwelt higher up in the mountains, nor less ready to lay down their lives in defence of it, they contended for a quarter of a century or more with the invaders who came into their land, pretending to a right to rule over them. But in this long period of resistance the chivalry of the Kabardas was gradually wasted, whereas army after army came out of the north as from a womb of men which was inexhaustible. These semi-barbarous knights had also to contend with a more advanced civilization; and nature besides had not come to their aid with those bulwarks of rock and forest with which she so fondly encircled the free homes of the highlanders. A half century ago, accordingly, they were finally obliged to succumb to superior numbers, though not to superior valor. But they came out of the contest with the honors of war, it being stipulated in their capitulation that they should retain their arms, and be still governed by their chiefs, on condition of acknowledging the supremacy of the czar. Gradually, however, as the foreign civilization got a foothold with its advantages of trade and its superior modes of tillage, the influence of the conquerors grew stronger. Their colonists, consisting mostly of Germans, pushed forward into the fertile and pleasant valleys. Many of the chiefs, long courted by gifts and pensions, were seduced into favoring the Russian ascendency; a species of militia was drafted among the warriors to assist in the subjugation of the other tribes; and the hot young bloods, captivated by the sight of the epaulettes and plumes of the imperial cavalry, allowed themselves to be enrolled in its ranks, and formed that splendid body of horse having the guard of the person of the empress in St. Petersburg.

Previously to his invasion of the territory of these Russianized Kabardians, Schamyl had made various attempts to incite them to throw off their yoke. He had sent emissaries to scatter among them his proclamations, urging them in glowing words to strike a blow for independence and for Allah; he had caused these to be followed by many of his most eloquent murids who preached in their valleys that new faith of the union of all believers in a holy war against the infidels which had taken such strong root among the rocks of the mountains; and finally he had despatched his zealous partisan Achwerdu-Mahomet at the head of an armed force to compel them to take sides with him. But the Kabardians who, formerly converted from paganism to Muscovite Christianity and afterward to Mahometanism, were not zealots in religion, turned a deaf ear to both proclamations and preaching, and even put Achwerdu-Mahomet to death. For alike despising the threats of

Schamyl, and fearing the artillery of the Russians, they determined to remain neutral.

The following is one of the proclamations referred to, and may be taken as a specimen of Schamyl's State papers.

"In the name of Allah, the all-merciful, whose gracious Word flows like the spring before the eyes of the thirsty wanderer in the desert, who has made us the chief pillars in the temple of his faith, and the bearers of the torch of freedom! Ye warriors of great and little Kabarda, for the last time I send to remind you of your oath, and to incite you to war against the unbelieving Muscovites. Many are the messages I have already sent, and the words I have spoken to you; but ye have scorned my messengers and have not regarded my admonitions. Therefore hath Allah given you over into the hands of your enemies, and your aouls to the sword of the spoiler; for the Prophet hath said,

"'The unbelievers who will in nowise believe shall God deal with as with the vilest of the beasts.'

"Say not in reply: we believe, and have

always held the doctrines of the Prophet holy. Verily, God will punish you — liars. Say not: we faithfully perform our washings and our prayers, give alms, and fast, as it is written in the Koran. Verily, I say unto you, for all this shall ye appear black-faced before the judgment-seat of Allah. The water shall become mud in your mouths; your alms, the wages of sin; and your prayers, curses. The true believer has the faith in his heart, and the sword in his hand; for whoso is strong in faith is strong in battle. More accursed even than our enemies are ye; for they are ignorant and wander in darkness; but the light of truth shone before you, and ye have not followed it. Say not: they have overpowered us and by their great numbers put us to flight. For how often shall I repeat to you the words of the Prophet when he says,

"'Ye faithful, though the unbelieving come against you by hosts, turn not your back to them; for whoso then turneth his back, even though in the thick of the fight, him shall the wrath of God smite, in hell shall be his resting-place, and verily the way thither is not pleasant!'

"Wherefore have ye doubted the truth of my mission, and listened rather to the threats of the enemy than to my admonitions? God himself hath said,

"'Rouse, O Prophet, the faithful to battle; for twenty of you standing fast shall overpower two hundred, and a hundred of you shall put to flight thousands of the unbelieving, for they are a people that have no knowledge.'

"God has made your way easy, for he knew that you were weak. Had ye joined yourselves in league with us, ye would never have become the slaves of the infidels, and their touch had never defiled you. But now is it not easy to wash yourselves clean of their dirt. Was it then I who united together the tribes of the mountains, or was it rather the power of God working through me with wonders? The Prophet saith,

"'Though thou hadst squandered on them all the treasures of the earth, thou couldst not have united their hearts; but God hath made them one, for he is almighty and allwise. O Prophet, with God and the faithful on thy side, thou hast nothing to be afraid of.'

"Believe not that God is with the many! He is with the good, and the good are always fewer than the bad. Look about you, and see if my words be not true. Are there not fewer noble war-steeds than bad ones? Are there not fewer roses than weeds? Is there not more mud than pearls, and more lice than cattle? Is not gold scarcer than iron? And are we not better than the gold, and the roses, and the pearls, and all the horses and cattle put together? For all the treasures of the earth pass away; but we are immortal. But if the weeds be more numerous than the roses, shall we instead of rooting them out, suffer them to grow and choke the noble flowers? And if the enemies be more than we, shall we, instead of hewing them down, suffer them to take us in their snares? Say not: the enemy has conquered Tscherkei, and destroyed Akhulgo, and taken possession of Avaria. When the lightning strikes one tree, do all the others bow their heads and cast themselves down, lest it strike them also? O ye of little faith! would that ye might take example from the green wood! Verily, the trees of the forest might shame you if they had tongues. Or when the worm destroyeth one kind of fruit, do then all the other kinds perish for fear lest they may be pierced through also? Wonder not that the unbelievers multiply so rapidly, and send army after army to take the place of those whom we cut off; for I say unto you that thousands of mushrooms and poisonous weeds shoot up out of the earth, while one good tree is growing to maturity. I am the root of the tree of freedom; my murids are the trunk; and ye the branches. But think not because one branch rots the whole tree will go to ruin. Verily, the rotten branches will God lop off, and cast them into hell-fire; for he is a good husbandman. Repent, therefore, and return to the ranks of those who fight for the faith, and my grace and protection shall overshadow you. But if ye continue to trust to the enticing words of the flax-haired Christian dogs rather than to my warnings, I will surely fulfil that which Khasi-Mollah long ago promised you. Like dark clouds shall my warriors overshadow your aouls, and take by force what you refuse to kindness; blood shall mark my path, and terror and desolation shall follow in my footsteps; for where words do not suffice, deeds shall."

Of the Russian proclamations in the Caucasus, on the other hand, the following, issued in reply to Schamyl's, may serve as a specimen.

"In the name of God, the almighty.

"The Adjutant-general, commander of the Caucasian corps, and chief of the civil government of the Cis and Trans-Caucasian territories, to the Khans, Beys, Cadis, Effendis, Mollahs, and to all the people of Daghestan and Tchetchenia.

"The commotions and bloodshed which during so many years have taken place among the Caucasian mountaineers have attracted the most serious attention of our lord, the emperor; and his Imperial Majesty has resolved this year to introduce the reign of peace and prosperity into all these unhappy districts. To carry this purpose into execution fresh troops have arrived, and in case of need still greater numbers can be drawn from the terrible hosts of Russia. And how numerous and powerful are her armies, those of you who have been in that country can best tell.

"Ye inhabitants of Daghestan and Tchetchenia! I assure you that these troops have in nowise been sent to root out the doctrine of Mahomet and to destroy his people, but simply for the punishment of Schamyl and his followers. For he is a shameless deceiver, who from purely personal motives, from the desire of self-aggrandizement and the love of dominion, has stirred up the tribes to revolt, and exposed them to all the horrors of war; who seeks himself to avoid every danger, while he delivers you, deluded ones, to death; who preaches equality of rights and abolition of all hereditary rights of property simply to get possession himself of the inheritances of your khans and beys; who fills your aouls with his murtosigators, who spare neither the lives nor the property of the innocent inhabitants; who lays on your settlements the burdens of his taxes and the hateful yoke of his despotism; who calls himself your protector and defender, while everywhere his presence is marked by death and desolation. So, for example, was it in Khasikumuck, Avaria, and Andi, in the Sechamschal district, and in Itchkeria, where he acted such a faithless and inhuman part towards the inhabitants of the aoul of Zoutera, sparing neither the aged, nor women, nor children. In place of your ruined prosperity he gives you nothing but false and delusive promises, as when he encouraged you with the hope of the speedy appearance of a Turkish army for your relief, whereas the sultan has just renewed to us his word never to interfere in the affairs of the Caucasian tribes, in opposition to their rightful emperor.

"Ye people of Tchetchenia and Daghestan! Soon will the Russian army appear in your midst. And I repeat to you that our troops will come only to deliver you from the yoke of your oppressor, to protect the weak, and those who turn from the error of their ways with repentance, as well as all those who have risen in revolt against the power of the despot. In the name of the great ruler of men, the emperor of all the Russias, who has delivered all power into my hands to punish the fomenters of strife as they deserve, but who nevertheless desires to throw over their offences the covering of his gracious forgiveness, do I promise full pardon to all those who by word or deed have labored for the cause of Schamyl, provided they now come to me with tokens of repentance and submission. I promise that all necessary means shall be taken for the preservation of your faith, of your mosques, of your customs and usages, and of the rights of property of all those who will now present themselves before me and take the oath of subjection and fidelity. All these their rights and privileges shall be placed on secure and ever-enduring foundations.

"But at the same time I inform you that all the aouls and tribes who join the party of Schamyl and oppose themselves to our rightful authority shall be subjected to the most terrible punishments. The same shall be inflicted also on all those who seek to retire into the mountains, and all those who, having fled thither, do not immediately return to their former habitations. And these habitations likewise shall be razed to the ground.

"As to the tribes of Akuska and Zudakera, the conditions on which their submission will be accepted will be made known to them by the commander of the forces in Daghestan.

"Ye people of Tchetchenia and Daghestan! In this year will your destiny be decided. It depends on yourselves. Choose! In case you submit yourselves to the rightful and beneficent rule of Russia, you will receive the inexpressibly great gift of the grace of our lord the emperor, who watches equally over the happiness and prosperity of all his subjects. But if you obstinately continue in your errors, and place yourselves in the ranks of our enemies, you will share in the punishment inflicted on Schamyl, and will be torn in pieces by the claws of the Russian eagle, which at the same time appears at the rising of the sun and where it goes down in the west, and which wings its flight over Elbrus and Kasbek as though they were mere mole-hills."

XXXIX.

HIS INVASION OF THE KABARDAS.

The black cloud of vengeance, though so small as not to be noticed by the Kabardians, was now gathering in the south-east. Schamyl, surveying the posture of affairs in the spring of 1846, with the eye of a warrior who was at the same time a prophet, saw that the concentration of Russian troops was mostly in the fortresses of Temir-Chan-Chura and Grosnaja; that Woronzoff was busy looking after his kreposts and his stanitzas; and that consequently there was an opening for himself by means of fast galloping to break through the enemy's line, and make a raid in the Kabardas. It was an inspiration of genius to conceive the plan; it would require the boldest riders in the world to execute it.

But notwithstanding the loss of Dargo, the year preceding, "Sultan Schamyl," as the mountaineers sometimes fondly called him, had attained to such an influence that he was now at the head of the largest force which had ever been mustered in the highlands. Among the tribes of the western Caucasus, their proudest chiefs, Guz-Bey, and Dschimbulat, had never been able to raise a troop for crossing the Kuban of more than four thousand riders; Scheik Mansur, the Schamyl of the eastern Caucasus in the preceding century, and Khasi-Mollah had never taken the field with upward of eight thousand; nor had the Russians in their hostile incursions, as at Akhulgo and Dargo, assembled under their eagles a greater force than from twelve to fourteen thousand. But the Imam after all the losses of the preceding years had now under him no less than twenty thousand warriors, a large proportion of them cavalry, and waiting only his order to spring into their saddles.

In the beautiful month of May, when nature in bud and full leaf throughout the mountains inspired the breast of the warrior as well as of the husbandman with hope,

Schamyl set forth for the Kabardas. The week before, the highlands lay as peaceful in the midst of the spring's blossoming as they had under the protecting mantle of the winter's snows. The steed was cropping the first tender blades of grass in the vale, long unaccustomed to the bit and saddle which hung suspended against his master's wall; while the Lesghian himself was sitting listless at the door of his sakli apparently basking without a thought of war in the genial beams which shine in the time when the singing of birds is come, and the voice of the turtle is heard in the land.

But suddenly there was a hot riding of messengers from one end of the little empire of the Imam to the other. In a week all the men of Himri, Akhulgo, and Dargo, the riders of Arrakan and Gumbet, Avaria and Koissubui, Itchkeria and Salatan, the dwellers on the four branches of the Koissu and the still blood-stained banks of the Aksai, Lesghians, Tchetchenians, and warriors of Daghestan, tribes of different origin and speaking various dialects, but freemen all, were in the stirrup, shaskas at their sides, and millet at their saddle-bows.

Two rivers flowed between their land and the Kabardas; and across their war-path ran two lines of hostile fortresses. Among these latter was the strong-hold of Wladikaukas, besides others scarcely less impregnable; and in them all lay an army of seventy thousand troops well armed and ready for service. In the intervals between stretched the settlements of the Cossacks; and beyond, the Kabardians themselves had been born warriors, and still retained their arms. On the other hand, Schamyl had no artillery, and no regular convoys of provisions and ammunition. Without fortresses, depots, or communications of any sort to fall back upon in case of need, he would in fact have nothing behind him to rely upon, but only that which was before. It would be therefore a dash at a venture, and with, for order of march, "The devil take the hindmost."

But the Imam was conscious of his strength, and was justly proud of his twenty thousand men of the mountains, every one of whom held in contempt the plains below and all they that defended them. Seeing beforehand both the victory and the way of escape, he confidently set forward. It was at the season of the year when the banks of the rivers were filled full from the melting of the snows in the mountains; but the horses swam where they could not ford the currents. To no purpose was it that the Cossack, seeing from his tall look-out the approach of the foremost riders of this host, lighted his beacon, or that the sentries of the kreposts fired their alarm-guns. Schamyl rode down the Cossacks, plundered the stanitzas, and left behind the forts which were not carried amid the whirlwind of his first coming. There was no stopping; and before the garrisons along the line knew that Schamyl had come, he was gone; and when the Kabardians believed that the braggart who had threatened their land with plundering was shut up in his mountains six hundred wersts away, he was in their midst.

No less than sixty populous aouls of the Kabardians were plundered; twenty Cossack stanitzas were destroyed; and ravaging on either side the lands through which he passed, the Imam seriously threatened the strong places of Mosdok, Jekaderinograd, and Stavropol. It was easy galloping over the smooth valleys and softly rolling hills of the Kabardas; nor having once broken the bounds of the mountains were Schamyl's riders content to turn back their horses until they had watered them on the Kuban, and even filled with consternation the stanitzas on the still more distant banks of the Laba.

To retreat from these remote steppes in safety to the mountains was indeed a triumph. For the generals Freitag and Nestoroff, on hearing the news of Schamyl's incursion, had immediately mustered their battalions, and occupied the Terek to intercept his return; and the Cossacks, those of the Don, of Tchernomozen, and of the line, riding at full speed, had come in from the plains with a strength of several thousand lances. Schamyl well knew that he could not retire by the way in which he had advanced. But when the work of devastation and pillage was done, he suddenly turned his horses' heads south from Jekaderinograd; overran the Cossack colonies in that direction; and with a considerable number of Kabardians forced into his ranks, with his cruppers loaded with the booty of the plains, and his saddle-bows well furnished with both millet and mutton, regained the mountains. It was still the beautiful month of May when his riders unloosed their saddle-girths at the doors of their saklis; the time of the singing of birds was not past; nor had the voice of the turtle yet ceased in the land.

XL.

HIS SYSTEM OF GOVERNMENT.

But the one half is not told respecting the genius of Schamyl after the recital of his military exploits simply; for he is not more distinguished as a warrior than as a ruler and a lawgiver. Out of the heterogeneous materials of numerous independent tribes, separated from each other in many instances by blood-feuds, speaking various dialects, and having traditions and customs more or less differing, he has organized a form of society in which all these discordant elements have been brought into harmony. Where before there were tribes, there is now a State; where there were many warlike leaders and hereditary chiefs of clans, there is now one supreme ruler; in the place of usage and tradition, there is the reign of law and order; and instead of a resistance of clans fighting bravely but without concert, there is a well-organized system of defence, with concentration of powers and unanimity of action. It is an organization called forth by the exigencies of a state of perpetual war, and one wherein individual liberty is necessarily and rightfully sacrificed to the common independence.

The foundations of this militant state were laid on the rock of religious fanaticism, the cleft between the two sects of Omar and Ali having been finally cemented together in the new faith of the Sufis. This great work was begun by the predecessors of Schamyl, but to him is due the credit of having carried it on to perfection, until now the war of sects has been completely merged in the war against the common enemy, and hatred of the "blonde unbelievers" is synonymous with love of Allah and faith in the Prophet. Of this united church Schamyl is the head. He is acknowledged as the second great prophet and Allah's vicegerent, appointed to defeat his enemies and to maintain the liberty originally granted by him to the sons of the mountains. Twice in the year he is believed to hold direct communications with heaven, retiring for that purpose to the privacy of his inner apartments, or the solitude of some cave or retreat among the rocks. There for three weeks he performs his priestly worship with fasting, prayer, and the reading of the Koran, until at length he beholds in a vision the spirit of the Prophet descending out of heaven in the form of a dove, and receives from it the divine commands. On returning from his place of seclusion he delivers these to the assembled congregation of his murids and murschids, and exhorts them with the rapt eloquence of a messenger come directly from God to persevere in the holy war against the Muscovites. Awed by the solemn tones of his voice and by the almost supernatural shining of his countenance, the congregation accepts his words as the inspiration of the Almighty, and bows itself in prayer. Then going out of the mosque he chants a verse from the Koran, and harangues the multitude outside, who thereupon sing a hymn which is half a battle song, and drawing their shaskas swear anew fealty to the faith, and eternal hate against Russia. And finally, the ceremony over, all separate amid shouts of, "God is great; Mahomet is his first prophet; and Schamyl his second!"

The territory over which Schamyl bears rule is divided into provinces, districts, and aouls. A convenient number of aouls forms a district, and five districts a province. Over the latter are set governors who have a control in things both spiritual and temporal which is wellnigh supreme; but for the rightful exercise of which they are answerable to the Imam with their lives. Next in authority are the chiefs of districts, who are called naibs, and whose duties consist in maintaining a supervision over the inhabitants, collecting the revenues, raising recruits, settling feuds, and enforcing due obedience to the law of the scharyat. Finally, in every aoul resides a cadi, or elder, who is required to make reports to his naib of all important occurrences, to keep the peace, to deliver up persons accused of crimes, to promulgate the orders and proclamations of his superiors, and to keep swift horses constantly standing saddled and bridled for the instant despatch of messengers of State.

Every naib, moreover, is bound to maintain in his district an armed force of three hundred riders, to be raised in the manner following. Every ten houses furnish a warrior, the family from whom he is taken being free of all taxes during his lifetime, and the other nine being at the expense of his equipment and maintenance. This soldier is to be ready to march at the minute, and may not lay aside his arms even at night. In addition, every male from fifteen years of age to fifty is liable to be called out for the defence of his aoul, or, in extraordinary cases, for active service in the army. At the same time the horseman of every ten houses takes command of the men on foot from those houses.

Separate from his standing army Schamyl has also a guard constantly attached to his person, which is made up by selection from his murids. They are called by way of distinction Murtosigators. Into their number none are admitted save warriors of well-tried valor, zealous for the faith taught by the murschids, and devoted partisans of the Imam.

Called to the high office of guarding the person of their prophet, they must keep themselves pure from whatever in the world might tempt them to a neglect of duty, or even make life too dear to them. If unmarried, they must remain so; if married, they must have no intercourse with their families. They must exercise temperance in living, and strictly keep the scharyat. The extension of the new faith, the maintenance of the supremacy of the Imam, and the triumph of his arms over his enemies, must be the aim of their every thought and endeavor.

In number the murtosigators are about one thousand, and are organized on the decimal system, every ten having a leader, and every ten leaders again a superior, as is the case also in the regular army. They receive a regular monthly pay, besides a share in all spoils. In time of comparative peace, while one half of them keep watch over the life of the Imam, rendering access to him a matter of extreme difficulty, the other half act as lay preachers of his political Sufism; and in time of actual war, they are the soul of his army, caring not for their lives but only for his, leading the raid, covering the retreat, a strong wall of defence around the faithful, and the terror of the enemy, by whom not one of them has ever been taken alive.

In imitation of the grades of office in the Russian armies, Schamyl established a difference of rank among his own chieftains. Three of his most eminent partisans received titles corresponding to those of generals; and a number of his murids, especially the chiefs of the murtosigators, were made captains. At the same time these high officers were distinguished by decorations after the European fashion. The generals were authorized to wear on each breast stars of silver; the captains had silver plates of an oval form; and the chiefs of the guard who had distinguished themselves by acts of extraordinary heroism were presented with medals bearing complimentary inscriptions in the Arabic character. There were also various other rewards of military merit established, such as epaulettes of beaten silver, daggers with silver hilts, and ensigns decorated with fine needle-work. And to correspond with these marks of honorable distinction were instituted badges of disgrace, such as the patch sewed on the back, and the rag tied around the right arm. Finally, a system of military punishments was introduced, comprising various fines, imprisonment, and death.

For a revenue Schamyl does not depend, like his predecessors, on the fifth of the booty taken from the enemy, and the fines imposed for violations of the scharyat, but has introduced a regular system of taxation. A poll-tax to the amount of a silver rouble, or its value in kind, is levied on every family; one tenth of the produce of the land goes into the public treasury; the property of every person dying without direct heirs, falls to the government; and the wealth accumulated in the mosques and shrines, consisting of the gifts of the pious, has been applied to the uses of the State, the mollahs receiving regular pay in exchange, and the wandering dervishes, who lived on voluntary contributions, having either been incorporated into the army or driven out of the country. Economical in the use of his revenues and living himself in a style of simplicity scarcely superior to that of his comrades in arms, the Imam has accumulated considerable funds, and is known to have deposited in secret places in the woods of Andi and Itchkeria treasures of gold, precious stones, and various valuables. The sinews of his war are not indeed gold and silver, but love of freedom and hatred of the infidel; still he understands as well as the rulers of countries more civilized, that riches are a strong ally; and moreover he can neither issue paper-money nor live by borrowing. But while he has wisely laid up in store for the conduct of the war and the upholding of his government whatever could be saved by frugal and simple living, he has always dealt out with a liberal hand the means necessary for rewarding acts of extraordinary valor or self-sacrifice, for making converts to the faith of the Sufis, or for winning over to his side a hostile tribe or chieftain.

The mountaineers acknowledging the rule of Schamyl do not number more than about six hundred thousand, the entire population of the Caucasus being estimated at a million and a half. The forces of the Imam have never exceeded twenty thousand. On the other hand, the Russian army in the mountains during the last dozen years has consisted of from one hundred and fifty to two hundred thousand men of all arms. These have been distributed indeed throughout both Cis and Trans-Caucasia, a portion of them being occupied in vainly endeavoring to conquer the Circassians proper in the western extremity of the mountains, but a greater proportion, say from fifty to one hundred thousand, being concentrated along the line of the Tchetchenian and Lesghian highlands. According to the Russian ordnance accounts of the year 1840, their total expenditure of artillery cartridges was 11,344, and of musket cartridges 1,206,575. Large expenditure, and small result.

XLI.

RECENT EVENTS.

DURING the last few years the Imam has kept the Czar well at bay. Since the capture of Dargo, the Russians have made few incursions, and reported no more victories. And on the other hand, the mountaineers making only now and then a razzia, or storming a krepost, have been contented to allow the enemy the quiet enjoyment of his prison-houses along the line, on the condition of his not leaving them. Schamyl seems to be well aware that his best ramparts are the rocks, and his palisades the primitive forests. To leave these for the sake of attacking fortified places bristling with cannon, and which if captured he could not hold, would be a useless waste of blood too precious to be spilled without cause. And, besides, he must know that he is contending not only against superior numbers, but also a more perfect knowledge of the art of war, and that therefore his only hope of ultimate success can rest on the interposition of that Providence which guides the world's destiny.

At length that heavenly power seems to be coming to his relief. For nearly half a century he has been holding in his hand the keys of the great pathway from southern Russia to the East, despite the utmost efforts of the czar to wrest them from him. In vain did the emperor Nicholas visit the Caucasus to cheer on his troops; in vain did the grand-duke Alexander, the present emperor, take part in the campaign of 1850; or Prince Baratinksky in 1852 attempt by his bravery to overawe Tchetchenia. From Jermoloff to Woronzoff and Mouravieff the emperor has sent to the Caucasus his best generals, who have devised or put into execution every possible system of both attack and defence for the sake of destroying this nest of mountaineers; the banks of the Kuban and the Terek have been covered with Cossacks until their lances stand as thick as the river-reeds; ten thousand times in the year, it has been estimated, does the cannon roar through these valleys, and ten hundred thousand times does the musket ring; but the mountains stand firm; the hills are not shaken; the flag of freedom, though but a rag tied to a spear, still floats from the summits of Andi and the Solo-Tau; and Schamyl still holds the mountain path which leads from Russia to the valleys of Persia and the plains of Hindoostan.

England, comprehending at last that the progress of Russia eastward, if not checked, would at no very distant day threaten the security of her own dominion in Asia, has in concert with France commenced a war which, if carried to a successful and true issue, will bring about the evacuation of the Caucasus by the Russian arms, and shut on them, at least during the present generation, this gate of the Orient. Should the war stop short of this result, the subjugation of this strong-hold of liberty will not probably be postponed long beyond the decease of its present heroic defender; and the student of history will search in vain to discover the purposes of Providence to accomplish which this child of genius and of nature was raised up.

It is not strange, however, that Schamyl should not fully comprehend, as he appears not to do, the nature of the deliverance which would seem to be preparing for him. Attempts are said to have been made to induce him to adapt his policy to the peculiar state of the relations of eastern and western Europe, and to coöperate with the enemies of Russia by attacking her lines in the Caucasus now that they are beginning to be weakened from the suspension of the usual reinforcements. France has sent presents of muskets to the Caucasus, and England has despatched diplomatic agents. But hitherto the Imam has not departed from the line of policy which was traced out previously to the breaking out of the war in Europe, and with sole reference to the posture of affairs in the Caucasus. It is said, and probably with truth, that he distrusts the overtures of alliance made to him. For since the government of Great Britain refused to demand redress for the capture by the Russians of the "Vixen," an English vessel trading on the coast of Circassia in contravention, as was alleged, of their laws of blockade, and thereby virtually declined to acknowledge the rights and independence of the Circassians, the latter have lost all faith in that intervention of England in their favor which for a time they had been encouraged in entertaining. For the name of the great Napoleon, the sultan of the west,—for into what parts of the earth has his name not gone forth?—they cherish the most profound admiration; but they do not know his nephew, nor have they ever been brought into any relations whether of trade or diplomacy with France. Moreover, the words, "ally," and "protector," have become almost words of ill-omen in the Caucasus, from the fact that the Russians, like the Persians and the Turks before them, have always used these terms to mask their designs of interference and ultimate conquest. The wily Imam therefore distrusts the Franks though *dona ferentes*, and dreads lest they who should come into the mountains as allies might remain there as masters. He prefers to continue trusting in himself and Allah, and to let the unbelievers fight their own battles. Nor, indeed, is it quite certain that herein he does not act wisely.

It has been supposed by some, though without sufficient reason, that the recent restoration to Schamyl of one of his sons who had been taken away in his boyhood to Russia and there educated, has had some influence in rendering him more disposed to be on terms with his enemies. This interesting event occurred, however, in the course of a regular exchange of prisoners, and in the manner following.

His son, together with a ransom of forty thousand silver roubles, was demanded by Schamyl in return for the deliverance from captivity of two Russian princesses, the princess Tschattchavadse, and the princess Orbelian, with the children of the latter, all of whom had some months before fallen into the hands of some of his followers. This was finally agreed to, and the interchange was effected by Schamyl in person. Distrustful, however, to the last moment, he came to the appointed place of rendezvous on the banks of the frontier river Mitschik accompanied by a force of some six thousand warriors and several field-pieces. Then having taken up his position on the right bank while the Russians occupied the left, he sent forward another of his sons, Khasi-Mahomet, with thirty murids to escort the captives. At the same time a party of riflemen commanded by Major-general Von Nikolai advanced from the other side, having in charge Jamal Eddin, the son who was to be exchanged, and a carriage containing the ransom money. When then Jamal Eddin came down to the ford, the thousands of his countrymen who covered the neighboring heights set up a shout of thanksgiving, and chanted the *Estaphir Allah.* Then having crossed the river, he put on a Circassian dress, and in company with his brother and the Russian officers climbed the hill where, surrounded by his murids, and having a large parasol held over his head, sat the Imam. When the son who had been lost and was found approached, the heart of the venerable father was deeply moved; and stretching out his hand for the young man to kiss, he then embraced him, and wept.

The report of the interview, published in

Tiflis, states that Schamyl at the close of it, after having bowed courteously to the officers and thanked Baron Nikolai for the kindness with which he had treated his son, exclaimed, as if involuntarily, "Now I believe in the honor of the Russians." This, however, is doubtful.

The interview, it may be added, was memorable also from the circumstance that it was the first time since the year 1839 that any Russian is known to have seen the face of Schamyl. All present were struck with its expressiveness, as they also were favorably impressed by his noble and prepossessing manners.

THE END.

www.ingramcontent.com/pod-product-compliance
Lightning Source LLC
LaVergne TN
LVHW020238110826
845151LV00003B/965